PRINCESS ANNE AND HER HORSES

Judith Campbell

PRINCESS ANNE AND HER HORSES

BROCKHAMPTON PRESS

Other books by Judith Campbell

THE QUEEN RIDES
ANNE, PORTRAIT OF A PRINCESS
ELIZABETH AND PHILIP
HORSES IN THE SUN
WORLD OF HORSES
WORLD OF PONIES
FAMILY ON HORSEBACK

ISBN 0 340 16541 3

First edition 1972

Published by Brockhampton Press Ltd, Leicester
Printed and bound in Great Britain by
Fletcher & Son Ltd, Norwich
Designed by Douglas Martin
Set in 'Monotype' Ehrhardt

Contents

CHAPTER ONE

The will to win

Six weeks before the European Horse Trials Championships, held at Burghley on September 2nd–5th, 1971, Princess Anne went into hospital for a major operation. It must have been a bitter blow, for after a period of suspense, while the pundits weighed Anne's good performance at the Badminton Trials in the previous April against her and her horse's lack of experience in Three Day Events, she had been asked to ride for Britain as an individual – her greatest ambition to date.

Now it seemed, if not impossible, at least extremely remote that there could be any question of the Princess riding at Burghley, in a tough competition where peak physical fitness is as essential for the rider as the horse. But 'impossible' (like 'protocol') is not a word to which Princess Anne takes kindly.

Even Alison Oliver, who helps train the Princess and her horses, had given up hope of Anne being able to compete at Eridge, the final trial in August before Burghley, but when she went to see her in hospital to commiserate, only a short while after the operation, she found the patient sitting up in bed working out plans for a crash get-fit course. It took dedication, determination and guts, some of the same qualities that Princess Anne brings to her competitive riding and, combined with the great asset of being only twenty-one, it worked.

Eridge was not an unqualified success. Coming up out of the water Doublet jumped too big up a bank, landed too close to the rail on landing and stopped. Anne turned him on the bank and somehow he hurled himself over, but there wasn't enough room and he pecked and slipped

---

Eventing is a tough sport – even at the lower grades. Princess Anne pushes Collingwood on down the 'slide' at Tweseldown.

up on landing. It was something that could happen to anyone and detracted nothing from the obvious grit and ability of both horse and rider, and the objective was achieved. Anne was to be given her chance, not as a member of the British team, but riding for Britain as an individual entrant.

Burghley, the great Elizabethan house set among acres of park and woodland, provides the perfect setting for a top-class sporting event, but until that weekend in '71 the annual Three Day Horse Trial had not produced quite the same compelling magic as Badminton, nor caught on even with the eventing enthusiasts to quite the same degree. Several times previously the fixture had clashed with other big horse dates, and anyway eventing is a relatively new type of competition to the public, rapidly growing in favour with competitors, but less easy to televise, and popularise, than show-jumping, and seldom given much in the way of Press coverage. Until the previous April when Princess Anne and Doublet competed at Badminton and helped to put Horse Trials on the map, these were a comparatively unknown quantity to the majority of the ordinary sporting public.

But now Burghley was the scene of the European Championships, involving all the big names; against long odds the Princess *was* there, competing; the sun was shining, and the crowds came – breaking all records, and happy and relaxed in the excellently organised yet informal atmosphere that is the essence of a Horse Trial, however big and important.

---

above: When it comes to competing in public the Princess is always turned out correctly down to the last detail. Nowadays, with the important competitions she goes in for, that includes the full rig – top-hat, white stock, cut-away coat and white breeches, and a double bridle for her horse – for the dressage phase. Here she and Doublet are in the dressage arena at Burghley, where they scored the lowest number of penalty points to win this phase of the Event.

below: For exercising, as she was on this first time out with Doublet after leaving hospital, Princess Anne usually wears her favourite riding garb – shirt or sweater worn with American chaps or jeans. For strenuous schooling and jumping practice she finds breeches and boots more comfortable, and wears that well-known little 'sailing cap' to keep her hair in order.

The Princess is not in the least nervous and is probably happier and more confident when riding a horse than at any other time, and the mutual trust that develops between her and her competition horses is one of the secrets of her success. But naturally she gets strung up before a competition however well she may conceal it; she had no previous experience of competing at international level, and this was only her and Doublet's second full-scale Three Day Event; and the opposition was formidable. In all there were six former Olympic riders among the top eventers from the eight nations engaged, and the four members of the British team – which, with Britain as holder of the Olympic, World and European titles, started hot favourite – were all top-notch old hands.

Because the entry was filled to capacity, the dressage began on the Thursday. By the time that Anne, immaculately turned out, her hair piled up under the conventional top-hat, rode into the dressage arena on the Friday, last but one to go, there were a number of very good marks showing on the score board.

Dressage is a graduated system of horse training that results, or should result, in 'the harmonious development of the physique and ability of the horse', and the first phase of any Horse Trial is a set dressage test, on this occasion marked independently by three judges of world repute. To gain the least number of penalty points, the horse has to be free, light and cadenced in its paces; supple, active, undeviating on straight movements, correctly bent when moving on curved lines, motionless at 'halt' and with it all, calm, willingly obedient to its rider's lightest 'aids', giving the overall impression of 'doing it all on its own'.

This is not easy to achieve with a horse that has of necessity to be almost 'bursting out of its skin' with the well-being essential for the physically demanding phases that come after, and an animal which – like all of its kind – is uncomfortably sensitive to the intangible emotions, of excitement, stress or anything else, generated by a crowd and indulged in by its rider.

Someone experienced in top-class eventing ability has described Princess Anne as 'remarkably composed' when the big moment actually arrives. She needed to be on those days at Burghley, and she required also every ounce of the single-mindedness her upbringing and self-discipline have taught her to bring to the matter in hand, right from the moment she and Doublet embarked on the twenty-five or so memorised movements of the test.

Even to the uninitiated it looked good, and when the marks went up there was reason for Anne's grin of delight. Only 41.5 penalty points, 7.5 better than Muhin of the USSR, the runner-up – and leading the field at the end of the first phase. But dressage, important as it is, is only one part, and in most ways the least exacting, of a Horse Trial, and there was a long way to go yet – as a rough estimate, about eighteen miles and forty-three fences.

Saturday, and the sun still shining but not too hot – an important factor this for Anne and the other competitors, setting off in turn on the first test of endurance, about four and a half miles of roads-and-tracks around the woodland and park.

There is a series of numbered kilometre markers, but no one to set the pace or help gauge the time in hand. The pace has to be steady, a fast trot or mixture of canter and walk, taking the least out of the horse though fast enough to keep within the limit. On the second lot of roads-and-tracks some jump-off and run beside their horses for a while to conserve their strength.

No problems here for Anne and Doublet. A quick breather, and then on to the steeplechase course, two and a quarter miles and ten authentic racing fences.

It's one thing to race as one of a huddle of runners, with the thudding of many hooves, the acrid stench from a crowd of sweating horses; with the mud that flies in your face from the chap in front, the crash and cusses as old so-and-so goes through the top of the fence beside you, the glimpse of a horse's ears coming up on your right, the will to win that's the motive power of any racehorse worth its oats. It's another matter to take on a race on your own, where the fences look just as big but your only rival is the ticking of the judges' stop watches.

Princess Anne has an inherited love of speed – it's a joy to her to go off hello-bellow with a good horse – and an animal of Doublet's calibre and fitness would not require much urging, so probably the danger lay the other way. Go too fast, get carried away, dissipate too

much energy with still another six and a half miles of roads-and-tracks to go, this time with a sweating, blowing horse, before the most demanding phase of all, and you end up tackling that tough cross-country with what every rider dreads – a tiring horse that may still have the courage to go on but really lacks the physical ability.

So once again Anne had to gauge what normally comes only from experience, the right speed to produce the right score without taking too much out of her horse. And even when she knew there were 'no penalties' for the steeplechase, that only provided half the answer. The other half would appear during the four-mile, 1,324-yard gallop interspersed with thirty-three fences, yet to come.

The last of the roads-and-tracks behind her, another short breather while the vet inspected Doublet, and it was time to be waiting her turn at the start. The Queen was out on the course in her host's Landrover, ready positioned to make a dash from fence to fence for as much of the way as was possible, but Prince Philip was there to give his daughter, and the horse originally destined as a polo pony for himself, a good send-off. So were quite a proportion of the 20,000 spectators at Burghley that day, with the rest, like the Queen, way out in the country to cheer the Princess on.

In fact they cheered and applauded Anne the whole way round – and it's doubtful if she heard any of it at the time. That's something that comes to one afterwards. The specialised publicity attached to her competing is one of the difficulties the Princess has had to contend with, in a sport where distractions for horse or rider can prove disastrous. Those fences are built solid, they don't come apart like show jumps if your horse hits one, and while this makes for good jumping because the horses as well as the riders appreciate the fact, if there is a

---

above: Princess Anne and Doublet, on the cross-country course at Burghley, arrive at the Trout Hatchery, second time round – the scene of trouble for several other competitors in the European Trials.

below: And a nasty moment for Anne when Doublet slid coming up out of the water. But she slipped her reins to give him maximum use of head and neck for recovery, kept grip and balance so that there was no added weight on his loins, and they were up and away again within minutes.

bad mistake somewhere along the line that often means a fall, and sixty penalty points – plus any incurred in the ratio of one for every three seconds in excess of the Minimum Time.

So Anne would be oblivious to everything but the requirements of the moment – implementing preconceived decisions on how to tackle the problem fences, riding Doublet into each obstacle with sufficient determination to give him the security and confidence to take-off and meet it right, without being pushed out of balance – and always conscious of the vital question of speed.

In those European Championships one or two of the fences were not all that far short of Olympic standard, yet there are quite a number of ordinary riders who could negotiate them safely . . . in their own time. It takes the extra-ordinary horsemanship, and courage and precision, to gallop on over a course like that at a speed even to keep within the time allowed.

Princess Anne has an inbuilt sense of rhythm in her riding and a very firm seat, and both were in evidence and very necessary at Fence 27, the Trout Hatchery, which had already been jumped once. Six of the forty-five starters misjudged their timing and got a ducking there on the first round, and as Doublet landed up out of the water the second time round, he slipped, almost coming down on to his stomach. It was an awkward moment, worse to look at than to experience according to the Princess, but she didn't shift. She gave him rein to stretch out and recover himself, then a reassuring pat to restore confidence and they were off again, back in the cadence of their gallop. Six more fences to go. Then, those six behind them with no troubles, no troubles anywhere except for that one slip-up, and it was through the finishing flags with the second fastest time of the day. Only 18.8 time penalties (and even the fastest competitor of all, who took the course like a scalded cat, scored 4.4 over), and now it was a case of 17.8 points ahead, overall. A good day for Princess Anne, and a good day for Britain – with the British Team well in the lead and British riders holding the first six places.

Last phase, Sunday morning, show-jumping day, Doublet and all but one of the French horses passed fit by the vet, the sun still shining, the crowds packing the perimeter of the arena to capacity.

'As far as I'm concerned there is no other one . . .!' was Princess Anne's tribute to Doublet after Burghley. They are seen here in the show-jumping phase, demonstrating rider's and horse's ability to adjust to the different requirements of each stage of a Three Day Event.

Horse Trial show-jumping is not competitive in the more familiar sense. There's only one round, no jumping-off 'against the clock', and any faults, including those incurred for exceeding the tight Minimum Time, add to the overall number of penalty points. The phase is designed to show rider's and horse's versatility and fitness, in coping with this type of jumping after the strenuous efforts of the previous day. Judged against those of show-jumping proper, the fences are relatively small and the courses straightforward, but under the circumstances they are not easy. On that day none of the British Team went clear, and one member of both the Irish and the French teams clocked up 30 penalty points each.

Anne knew she could afford to have two fences down and still win, but nothing is a certainty at this game. She knows only too well that

horses are not machines, that they're as unpredictable as humans and just as capable of having an 'off' day, and trouble with the show jumps at Badminton in the previous spring had cost her and Doublet a possible place to give them fifth.

Anne wasn't going to leave anything to chance, but it was a fraught moment as she rode in to begin her round, and maybe she wasn't altogether prepared for the almost tangible waves of tension that flowed across the arena from one throng of spectators to the other. It could have added to her own tenseness and affected Doublet – as it had done at Badminton – and as they cantered through the start and on to the first fence she may have remembered how he had appeared a little stiff and at first jumped without his usual poise and gaiety. This time there was none of that, and any lingering anxieties about the water, the next to last jump, were scattered as they cleared it with feet to spare. Then, through the finish with a clear round to clinch the matter – the win that everyone was willing, and a thunder of cheering and applause to set the chestnut alight as his rider galloped him on a more than well deserved lap of honour.

It really was a day. Thirty-one finished out of forty-five starters, the British team right out ahead of the rest, British riders taking the first eight places – and Princess Anne beating the best in Europe with a final score of 60.3 (the runner-up with 98.1) to become individual European Champion. It added to it all that the Queen and Prince Philip were there to share the happiness of such a brilliant victory, made all the more exciting for being achieved with a home-bred horse.

A little bit of luck on the day must always play a part in a sport like eventing, but the individual European Championship of 1971 was won on true merit, and after a lot of hard work.

Princess Anne and Doublet at Burghley, the winners of the 1971 Individual European Horse Trials Championships. The Princess was ambitious as a child, and after she and Purple Star gained a creditable 8th place in their first-ever adult Horse Trial, her aspirations grew. But it's doubtful if she ever dared dream that, only three years on, she and the horse that learned the sport of eventing together, would be proudly carrying the Union Jack on the saddle cloth – representing Great Britain, and winning, in one of the toughest riding competitions in the world.

above: It must have been a wonderful moment for the Queen, as well as for Princess Anne, when she presented the Raleigh Trophy won by Anne and Doublet at Burghley in 1971.

right: Princess Anne with Doublet at Burghley in 1971, winner of the Individual European Eventing Championship.

below: Not long out of hospital – the last competition before Burghley '71 – Anne with Doublet at the Eridge Horse Trials.

CHAPTER TWO

First ponies

PRINCESS Anne had her first taste of riding when she was two and a half, just that much younger than the Queen who started at three, but in much the same way – on the back of a small Shetland under the guidance of her mother.

Anne needed no encouraging. From the time she could stand her favourite toys had been the Queen's old rocking-horse, and a wooden horse and cart belonging to Charles which she pedalled up and down the corridor outside the nursery; and she was certainly born into a horse-minded family. Her grandfather, King George VI, had been a fine horseman, and her grandmother, the Queen Mother, is still a steeplechasing enthusiast. The Queen loves horses and ponies regardless, rides whenever she can spare the time and is a recognised world authority on the complex subject of Thoroughbred blood-lines. Until he gave it up in 1971, polo was Prince Philip's absorbing sport, and spending Sunday afternoons up at Smith's Lawn watching her father play, even when she was so young she had to be tethered with a length of string to prevent her straying out among the ponies, has always been one of Anne's enjoyments.

To be taken to see the Highland and Fell ponies at Balmoral or the brood mares and foals at Sandringham, like visiting the riding horses at Windsor, quickly became an established ritual. While they were still quite young Charles and Anne went to occasional horse shows, and became familiar with such specialities as the spectacular Musical Ride put on by the Metropolitan Mounted Police during their annual show at Imber Court. A visit to the Royal Tournament was a special treat, with the highlight the Musical Drive of the King's Troop, Royal Horse Artillery, when the horse-teams gallop flat out around and across the

The Queen with Prince Charles, Princess Anne and Lord Snowdon at Badminton in 1960. This famous Three Day Event, held annually since 1949 at the Duke of Beaufort's estate in Gloucestershire, is always a favourite outing for the Royal Family. As a child Anne took the keenest interest in the proceedings, particularly the cross-country, but she's unlikely to have visualised herself tackling such stiff fences!

arena, drawing the creaking, swaying gun-carriages to criss-cross each other in a breathtaking exhibition of split-second timing. And every year from about six or seven years old upwards there was Badminton, the royal family's annual, private outing, where the crowds leave them alone to enjoy their day like everyone else.

Before she was old enough to take any part in royal processions herself, Anne enjoyed watching the state carriage horses, which she knew as individuals from visits to the Royal Mews, all decked out in the splendour of ceremonial trappings as they brought the carriages and coaches in and out of the central gateway of the Palace on state occasions. And she had an everyday view from the nursery windows of the squadrons of black Household Cavalry horses clattering by on their way to Whitehall, of the shining mounts of the police that help control the crowds gathered outside the Palace gates to watch the Changing of the Guard and of the splendid horse from the Mews that appears morning and afternoon at the Privy Purse Door, drawing a small black brougham and driven by a top-hatted coachman to collect and deliver the royal mail that goes 'by hand'.

The borrowed Shetland had proved conclusively that Anne was whole-heartedly pony-minded, and when she was three, William, ten hands high and a character in his own right, arrived for her and Charles from Ireland. This lively little pony was the prototype for the subsequent ponies in Anne's life. Attractive to look at but with no pretensions to being a costly 'show' animal, he was well-mannered, but no foolproof slug and well-suited to a child who never showed signs of nervousness and was soon demonstrating a preference for 'getting on with it'.

Obviously the first stages with William were an extension of what had begun with the Shetland, the pony being led out either by the Queen or by a groom on foot. But Anne, keen and confident from the start, soon progressed to going out on a leading rein beside the groom's horse.

The teaching of riding to children and the whole outlook on the subject has changed a lot since the Queen was a child. She remembers having great difficulty in persuading the trusted groom, who had charge of her and Princess Margaret, to let her 'off the lead' long after it was an unnecessary adjunct, but by the time her daughter was six Anne was coping with William without dual control.

Greensleeves, a 12.2 Welsh mare acquired principally for Charles, had appeared on the scene soon after William, and since in those years Prince Philip had time for horses over and above the polo practice and games, he and the Queen were able to enjoy family riding with their children in the park at Windsor.

Anne's professional instruction began when she and Charles started going to the Smiths' well-known riding school at Holyport, near Windsor, for occasional lessons that continued at intervals for a few

A family riding party at Windsor in 1957. The Queen with Betsy, the top favourite for many years, Prince Philip with Mele-Kush, the Akhal-Teke stallion given him by Mr Khruschev; Prince Charles with his Welsh pony mare, Greensleeves, and Princess Anne, then seven years old, riding her lively 'first' pony, William.

years. They were taught by Miss Sybil Smith who, up to the time she retired in 1971, must have been able to count her successful pupils in thousands, and who used to assist her father when he instructed the Queen as a child.

Miss Smith found Anne, like her mother, all out to learn everything she could about looking after ponies as well as riding them, and this continued the way she had been encouraged to help with her pony right from the beginning. The Queen always likes doing things for herself, and she made sure that, even if they'd been so inclined, the children never had a chance of looking on their ponies as riding machines, to be automatically produced ready accoutred when required and always taken away to be dealt with by someone else when the ride was over. The Queen taught her daughter how to catch and saddle up her pony and how to reverse the process and, with some supervision, Anne was soon coping with William and those that came after, much like any other child of her age that has a grass-fed pony. Anne's own determination to be as involved as possible has grown stronger with the years, and helped give her an otherwise impossible understanding of the various ponies and horses in her life.

Mayflower, the pony that superseded William and Greensleeves, was supplied from Holyport, then she too was replaced – by Bandit. This pony was, like the others, a good all-purpose type, who proved to be very good at gymkhana events and jumping. He was a typical 'pony' pony, cream coloured and reared on a Welsh farm, where working as a sheep 'looker's' mount on the hillsides increased his natural handiness and sure-footedness. He'd been spotted by a Wiltshire farmer's wife who 'has an eye' for a good pony, and she brought him to England to be schooled on. After only a month's training over jumps the pony was placed in a junior class at the Beaufort Hunter Trials, where he was seen and acquired for her young daughter by the Crown Equerry's sister. Bandit proved such a success that when he was outgrown he was sent on loan to Windsor, as a reliable, all-round pony, the right stamp for any child who wanted to start competing.

Anne was now ten and more pony-mad than ever. She'd been taught the rudiments of jumping by Miss Smith, and her decided taste for this side of the sport was furthered by Bandit, who took her over any of the small practice jumps that the Crown Equerry contrived for her at Windsor, with much willingness and mutual enjoyment.

Anne shared Bandit with Charles. Although the pony arrived with the reputation of going better for a girl, this was not borne out while he was at Windsor and he gave both children a great deal of fun. By then they were members of the Garth Pony Club and, while Charles left most of the rally-attending to his sister, they both started competing in a few of the gymkhanas and shows. To avoid publicity they always had to make a late entry on the day, which entailed going last of the competitors or thereabouts. Perhaps this was the first intimation Anne had that, even in riding, her position in life was likely to produce special difficulties.

However, neither she nor Charles allowed this particular one to deter them and they won quite a number of rosettes, mostly for jumping. Bandit inspired confidence because he was such an active, willing sort of animal, but there was no guarantee about his performance and he was fully capable of the behaviour that produced a win in the Bending Race for Anne and him at one gymkhana, but that sent him smartly, and literally into reverse at the line-up for the same event, at the next.

The competitive side was only a very small part of life with Bandit, and most of Anne's riding took place at Windsor, or on holiday in Scotland or Norfolk when Bandit was taken along too. A miniature cross-country course had been contrived around the Home Park at Windsor, and Anne and Bandit batted gaily around this, sometimes in

No need to worry about correct riding clothes when helping with Prince Philip's polo ponies, a favourite occupation in between chukkas at Smith's Lawn, Windsor.

181
171

above left: In the early days Anne and High Jinks enjoyed competing in the pairs class of a Pony Club Hunter Trial.

below left: Hello-bellow across country between jumps.

above: Anne was adept at boxing ponies and then hitching up the trailer.

the company of a party of children and ponies imported for the purpose. In the Easter holidays some form of mounted competition, a miniature Hunter Trial or its like, was sometimes organised by the Crown Equerry, enjoyable events that, to the Queen's embarrassment, were usually won by her daughter. But these successes weren't just due to a good pony and a familiar course. Great pains were always taken to organise new fences for such occasions, and most of the competitors were drawn from children already familiar with riding in the Park. Anne was likely to win because she has inherited the streak of determination that, in a few short years, turned her father from a mediocre rider into a high-goal polo player of world repute. It was a foretaste of the temperament that is essential for the standard of competition in which Princess Anne is now finding such success.

In public Prince Charles and Princess Anne, seen here with Bandit in 1963, were always turned out neatly dressed like other members of the Pony Club in jodhpurs, tweed jackets, Pony Club ties and badges . . . and hard black velvet riding caps!

CHAPTER THREE

High Jinks

On the sad day that Bandit, undeniably outgrown, departed back to the family that had supplied him, Prince Charles' interest in riding waned. He was finding plenty of new occupations at school, and there had always been the slightly discouraging realisation that his younger sister was that much keener, and better, than himself – and she was seldom backward in handing out advice! Charles came into his own again with horses about two years later, when a new-found enthusiasm for polo was given every encouragement by Prince Philip, but in the meantime he left ponies to Anne, whose zest for riding and competing was growing apace.

The arrival of High Jinks, a brown, 14.2-hand Irish pony, schooled by the same farmer's wife who discovered and trained Bandit, was a turning-point in Princess Anne's riding career and, in some ways, in her life apart from the sport.

This was the autumn of 1962 when Anne was twelve. She was an outdoor, tomboyish type of girl, self-confident, self-contained, a bit bossy and happiest when riding or merely messing about round the stables. Up to about this age the inevitable restrictions that are an ingredient of royal life had not bothered her particularly. Without personal comparisons to go by, she had accepted them as just part of life, but now she was getting restive. Subconsciously she had perhaps always felt that Charles, as the elder, as a boy and as Heir to the Throne, had the edge on her, and that she must always be out to prove she could keep up. He had gone away to prep school, and now was well embarked on an even more comprehensive 'outside' life at Gordonstoun, while she was still at home being taught by a governess. And in addition, it irked Anne to feel that there was someone there who always knew exactly where she was and what she was doing.

left:
Anne with High Jinks correctly accoutred for competing in public in 1965.

above:
By the time she was nineteen Anne had perfected the art of catching and leading four horses back to the Balmoral stables.

Up to then riding and ponies had been an absorbing hobby, but had meant little more to Princess Anne than to any other child with the same interest and capabilities. Now Jinks and life round the stables began to represent freedom, even if at that stage she seldom rode entirely alone. And deep down was the germ of the thought that still spurs her on – here was the means of proving to herself, and to the world at large, what she could do as herself, irrespective of who she was. If she could ride well and make a success of it, then it would be because she could *ride* . . . but not because she was Princess Anne.

There was no reason, except for deliberate parental preference, why Anne should not have had a fully 'made' pony, a top-of-the-mark brilliant animal that would act as schoolmaster and, given a bit of luck and the right tuition, whiz its owner into the winning echelon in whatever side of junior competing she wished to make her mark, in the shortest possible time. But there would have been no real challenge, nothing for Anne to get her teeth into, and the Queen and Prince Philip showed a shrewd understanding of their daughter's mentality and needs when they bought her High Jinks.

The pony had a nice, generous temperament and had been well schooled, but was only five years old and almost a complete novice. He had been hunted a few times, and in the April of that year jumped clear in the Working Pony Class at Badminton – a performance that interested Colonel Miller, the Crown Equerry, who had been keeping an eye on Jinks for some months. After competing at the White City in that July the pony was recommended to the Queen, and she agreed he should go to Windsor on trial for Princess Anne.

---

above: It was those rides in the parks at Windsor, at first in the company of her parents, later under the watchful eye of the Crown Equerry, sometimes in the company of other children, as she grew older more often on her own, that furthered Anne's inherent delight for galloping and riding across country.

below: There's a Royal Family ritual for thanking their horses and ponies with a titbit, usually a piece of apple or carrot, after a ride. Anne is including her friends' ponies in the general handout, after returning to the Middle Court in the Windsor Mews at the finish of a scamper all together round the park in 1964.

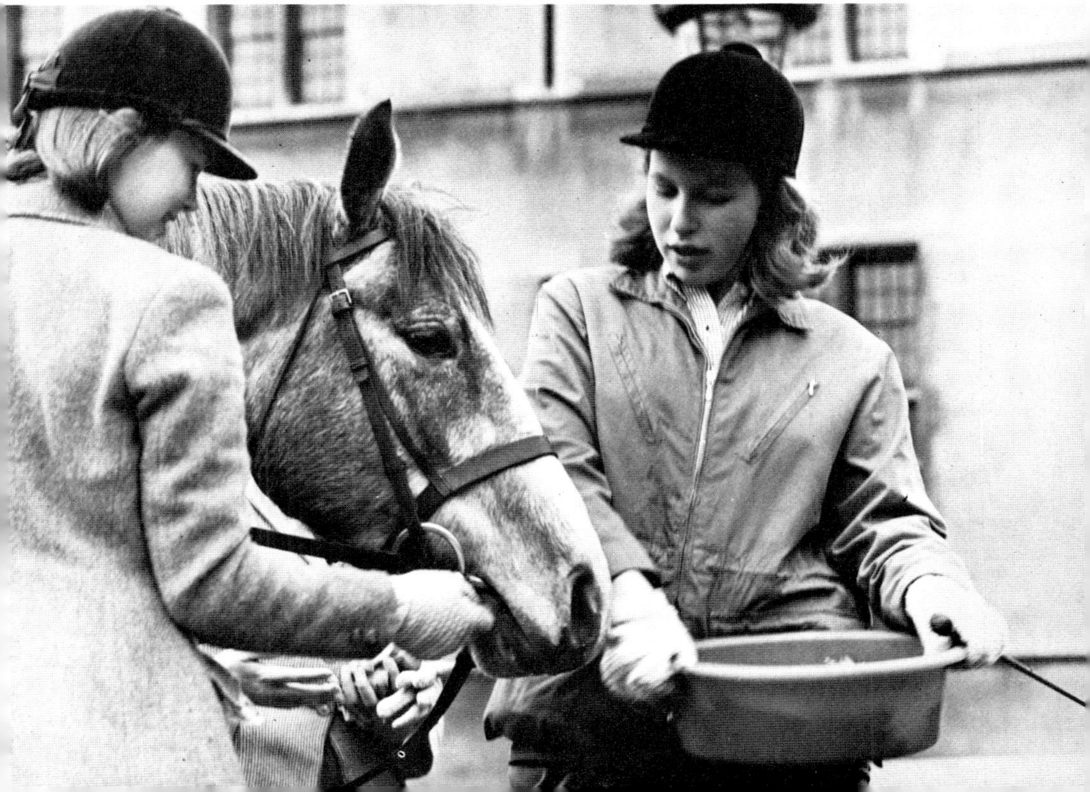

Jinks made an immediate good impression and his future owner was delighted with him, but before going finally to Windsor and while the royal family were on holiday in Scotland, the pony furthered his education by attending a Pony Club Camp, and competing in a Novice Junior Event and a Hunter Trial at both of which he again jumped clear. Obviously the material was there, and now it was up to Anne to develop it.

Sensibly the competing side was not rushed, and time was taken for rider and pony to get to know each other. Equally sensibly Jinks was not kept in and corned up, but lived out for part of each day, grazing with Andrew's Shetland, Valkyrie, for company. When he came in, either before a ride or, as he was trace-clipped, at night during the winter, Jinks inhabited one of the loose-boxes that are built round three sides of the Middle Court, that part of the Windsor Mews where the Queen's riding horses and ponies are kept.

During the weeks of termtime Anne's pony was exercised by a girl

Princess Anne's pony, High Jinks, (*right*) enjoying the Scottish forage at Balmoral in the company of the Queen's young horse, Benbow, and Andrew's Shetland, Valkyrie. All the riding horses are given freedom at grass as often as possible, and the ponies are always kept out.

groom, but when the Queen is resident at Buckingham Palace, which she is for most of the year, the family go to Windsor for every possible weekend, as well as for the Easter holidays. And on every available moment at these times Anne made for the great wooden door set in a high stone archway, that leads from the green expanses in front of the Castle through to the Mews.

Even when she was not actually riding Jinks there was always plenty going on to hold her interest. The stabling was built, in Victorian times, originally to house 120 horses, and although many of the old-fashioned stalls have been converted into capacious loose-boxes, and others in the Top and Lower Courts into space for storing fodder or accommodating cars, there is still room for a large number of animals. In summer, at any rate, the Mews was, and remains, almost full up.

There were the innumerable polo ponies that still clatter to and from exercise with their girl grooms, in those days eight or ten of them from Prince Philip's 'Yard', now almost exclusively those belonging to the Household Brigade, who have their Polo Club just inside the main entrance; usually there would be two or three of the royal riding horses, returned from the Park via the undulating, inviting and dead straight verges of the Long Walk; perhaps a young animal being taken out by the Rough Rider (who schools the young horses) for training, or Bussaco, the Portuguese stallion later loaned to a stud, being led across to take his daily exercise on a lunge in the covered school; and most mornings Anne's young brother Andrew, then a little boy, would appear with his nursery-maid to look at the horses or be led out on Valkyrie. Sometimes there were new arrivals to inspect, maybe a horse presented to the Queen by some foreign Head of State, or one of the 'home-breds' from Sandringham, come to make its début as a possible polo pony for Prince Philip. And at Easter there are always a team or so of the famous Windsor Greys, brought down from London for the royal procession up the race-course that precedes each day's racing at the Royal Ascot meeting. Along with them come young animals, their dark grey coats not yet whitened with maturity, that will benefit from being driven out in the Park and into the traffic, to teach them the impeccable manners and steadiness essential before they can be trusted to pull their weight on a ceremonial occasion.

For Anne there was always the hope of snatching a ride on something other than her own pony, for even as a child she liked to try out anything she could, and was quite confident of being able to cope. Pride, the horse that King Hussein of Jordan presented to the Queen in 1958, was one of Anne's first second-strings. She rode him at, and won, a Best Turned Out Horse Class in the Windsor Show, and Pride was likely to be her choice if, as occasionally happened, she slipped down to the stables during the grooms' lunch hour to help herself to a partner for an impromptu gallop in the Home Park.

As a teenager Princess Anne enjoyed Pride's gaiety, found his 'spooking' at strange objects amusing, and still laughs when he stands in the stable lolling out his tongue. Pride was given to the Queen by King Hussein of Jordan in 1958 and, always a favourite, is still in use at Windsor.

By the time she was fourteen, within reason Anne could take her pick of the stables, and this liking for proving that 'she could do it too' saved her from the pitfall of becoming a one-pony-only rider, and helped her develop into the true horseman she has become.

The Windsor Mews is a friendly place where Anne found the atmosphere of a workaday private family stable entirely to her liking, and with no hint of the pomp and circumstance of the Royal Mews in London – where the State horses, the magnificent collection of coaches and carriages, the priceless sets of ancient harness and saddlery presented from many countries in all parts of the world, are of historic interest and put on show to the public.

She liked to chat to the grooms in the warmth of the tackroom, where unused saddlery adorns one of the walls, but where otherwise almost everything is in everyday service. And unlike many children of well-to-do families, Anne had no selection of tack of her own. Both she and Charles had saddles made to the approved Pony Club Pattern, presented by the County Borough of Walsall, and bridles given by the Loriners' Company, whose Honorary Freedom she was to be happy to accept, later on, in March 1972. In those days her stirrups were of a quick-release safety pattern, and she rode Jinks in a vulcanite-mouthed half-moon Pelham bit.

Anne and Jinks got to know each other in the perfect riding conditions of the Windsor Parks, walking and cantering along the innumerable grassy tracks that criss-cross the Great Park, or galloping on that favourite straight up by Smith's Lawn, with Colonel Miller or a groom for company, or jumping round the cross-country course in the Home Park, where the variety of little fences had been increased to thirty-six in all. Jinks showed a dislike of ditches and water that had to be overcome, but otherwise co-operated, coping with equal enjoyment with obstacles across country or with the practice show jumps that were erected close by the Castle golf-course during the Easter holidays. And as time and the competing progressed, a dressage arena was added to the practising amenities.

The weather never puts off any member of the royal family, and frost and snow are almost the only conditions that defeat Anne when it comes to riding outside. At Windsor even these do not deter her, or the

Leg and body positions are not quite correct, the hands are a little far up the pony's neck. High Jinks could never be a Doublet – but as Anne, aged fourteen, was jumping her pony round the miniature cross-country course at Windsor, there was evident much of today's determination, sensitive hands and mutual confidence with her mount.

Queen, because they can go in the big riding school that is connected to the three stabling courts by a covered passageway.

When the family go to Balmoral on holiday, from around the second week in August until towards the end of September, they take some of the inhabitants of the Windsor Mews with them. One or other of the Queen's favourites goes along, possibly a polo pony for Prince Philip to hack, and maybe a pony or so for the younger boys. Jinks still goes, as he did in those early days, but is now corned up until he can hardly keep a hoof on the ground, to partner Anne when her riding is around the home estates, strictly for pleasure only.

Three or four ponies used for stalking live in a row of stalls in the small range of grey stone stabling at Balmoral, and the riding animals from Windsor inhabit loose-boxes close by. They usually spend part of each day turned out, and through the years Princess Anne has taken on the job of bringing them in and putting them out later, gradually perfecting her technique for coping with increasing numbers on her own. It's always headcollars only; she chooses Jinks to ride bareback and, by a complicated system of hitching each animal to a different place on the fence and collecting it again once she is mounted, now manages three or four together without any outside help.

Queen Victoria was a great one for exploring her beloved Scottish hillsides on the back of a Highland pony, and the Queen enjoys riding on the hill too. But Anne always considers trotting one of the least enjoyable paces, and since anything faster is 'out' on the rough tracks winding through heather and past peat hag, she prefers to ride down

Anne, leading Jinks out of the Middle Court at Windsor to put him back in the field after a ride. The Queen likes doing things for herself, and right from the start Anne entered into the life of her ponies apart from the actual riding.

by the river where there are some jumps, or on the flat ground surrounding the castle or beside the golf-course, where the Queen or Princess Margaret sometimes join her for a gallop.

Jinks still usually goes to Sandringham after Christmas with one of the Queen's horses. If weather permits, Anne then takes him along the rides cut through the Sandringham woods – where she continued getting to know him in the early days – or out on to those unploughed expanses of grattens (stubble) where she originally discovered that her pony, when he likes, has a turn of speed to match her mother's horses.

Back at Windsor Anne and Jinks continued to attend the Garth Pony Club rallies and then embarked on their first competitions, mostly in the pairs class in Pony Club Hunter Trials. In this way both rider and pony had partners to inspire confidence in their initial efforts, and they soon began to meet with some successes. By the Easter holidays of 1964 these included a first, a second and a third at various Pony Club competitions. There was also the odd gymkhana, with a novice show-jumping class or two and some rosettes here as well, and it became clear that Anne was increasingly competitively-minded and had the right animal with which to further her ambitions.

Jinks was proving a real all-rounder, handy and keen in whatever he was asked to do, but without ever hotting-up unduly and obviously possessing innate pony cleverness at extricating himself from awkward situations. He was not the sort of animal to do it all on his own, but needed riding, and then responded confidently to anything within his scope that his rider asked.

He was also very soon enjoying Anne's liking for speed, and for amusements such as the paper-chase, organised through Windsor Great Park when twenty children or so and ponies, with a sprinkling of mounted grown-ups in case of need, met behind the polo pavilion at Smith's Lawn one Saturday morning. Anne with Jinks and the Rough Rider with Benbow took their turn as hares, and provided a good gallop, as well as a network of true and false trails over about eight miles of muddy tracks and open heath, with only a couple of pre-arranged halts as breathing-spaces. It was a good day enjoyed by all, and for Anne another taste of the kind of partnership with pony or horse that she instinctively achieves.

In 1964 it was with different horses, but the enjoyment is the same – the Queen and Princess Anne in a gallop together across a big field of grattens in Norfolk. They often ride by themselves and do not always confine their activities to the boundaries of the estate.

The previous year there had been another of those miniature Horse Trials round the Home Park – again won by the Princess – and from the time she went to school gradually this aspect of competing, at first at its lowest standard, took over from the straightforward galloping and jumping of Hunter Trials. Maybe even then it was, characteristically, the greater challenge that appealed.

In April 1964 Anne took Jinks to compete in the Novice Class, fifteen years and under, of a Pony Club Horse Trials, one of the first public events of its kind they had attempted – and only seven years before that then undreamed of victory at Burghley.

It was an atrocious day with heavy squalls that made the going so bad the dressage arena had to be resited after the start, and the whole affair was soon running one and a half hours late. Cars, ponies, parents and children were all ploughing around in the mud. There were ponies with long shaggy coats, and a few with clipped-out, shining ones; ponies with ewe-necks and depressed expressions; workmanlike ponies, like their owners apparently oblivious of the elements; and . . . just ponies. A sprinkling of the competitors rode into the dressage on a moderately straight course; there were those whose mounts enlivened the proceedings with an unlawful buck or two, and the small, despairing rider, with a young pony that insisted on completing the test with its head screwed round to view the judges' Landrover with unfounded suspicion. All in all it was a very typical day.

As usual Anne went last, after a preparatory 'school' in the pouring rain and under the watchful eye of Mrs Gold, the Olympic Dressage rider who was District Commissioner of the Garth Pony Club and had been giving all the members a little helpful advice in the preceding weeks.

The Princess knew as much of dressage, and cared as little for it, as the majority of children of her age who are addicted to galloping and jumping. A dressage test was part of the type of competition she wanted to do, so it was only good sense to do one's best, but it would be quite a while before she would understand and accept the real whys and wherefores of this form of basic schooling.

It was not one of the days she and Jinks were to be 'in the money'. The pony, unappreciative of a double bridle, appeared to be resisting and somewhat 'wooden' in his responses, and at one stage his rider forgot her way. The marks were average, and despite a clear round over eight tricky little cross-country fences, a refusal in the earlier show-jumping phase ensured they would not be among the winners. Yet what stuck in the mind of the onlooker was the overall quietness of her riding in the dressage; the free manner in which she had Jinks going round all but that one show jump, and her usual *joie de vivre* and very apparent enjoyment, despite the long wait and being soaked to the skin, of the muddy gallop and jumping across country. And as Anne rode off happily squelching through the mud to box Jinks for the return journey, Mrs Gold expressed the wish that she could have the opportunity of getting really to grips with such potentially promising material.

Oddly enough, and indirectly, Mrs Gold's aspiration was to be fulfilled in the years to come when the Princess was already on the road to success. For Mrs Gold owns the stables in Berkshire where Alison Oliver, who came originally to work for her, keeps Princess Anne's horses and helps her with her combined training.

CHAPTER FOUR

Schooling and eventing

WHEN Princess Anne went to boarding school in the autumn of 1963, for the first and only time in her life she was able to become just one in a crowd, one schoolgirl among the 300 others attending Benenden School in Kent. And for the next five years when she rode during term-time at a well-known near-by riding establishment, she was taught with a class of other young riders, also for the first time – apart from the occasional Pony Club rally. Anne enjoyed both experiences and extracted everything she could from them.

At school she seized on the freedom provided by comparative anonymity, joined in the activities with enthusiasm and made a number of good friends. But although she liked any game, with the exception of netball, or any diversion that brought a chance of exercise outdoors, riding remained the one real, deep interest. The once-weekly sessions of riding instruction in the company of a mere eight companions were also a relief from the only aspects of school life to which Anne never became quite inured – the being surrounded always by hordes of people, and the, to her, 'staggering' volume of noise.

It was decided that it would be easier for Anne to settle at school if there were initially no distractions such as riding, but this was soon amended and after the first term Jinks spent each one at Moat House, the riding school his owner then attended.

By good luck Moat House was not only a first-class riding school conveniently close to Benenden School, but it is run by Mrs Hatton-Hall who is a Combined Training enthusiast. As Cherry Kendall she was a well-known competitor in Horse Trials, rode her own animal, Bright Prospect, at Badminton, and has for some years been on the

Senior Judges Dressage Panel up to the high standard of Prix St Georges.

Inevitably the Moat House atmosphere fanned Princess Anne's budding interest in Horse Trials, but to begin with there was a certain amount of unlearning to do before she could take even the first steps towards Combined Training as such. She arrived with a one hundred per cent enthusiasm for riding and getting on with it; and she had excellent balance, sensitive hands and the courage and ambition to get on to the back of any horse or pony in sight . . . if she was allowed to. But she rode with an old-fashioned length of rein and stirrup, and when it came to jumping there was more than a hint of the 'backward seat' of times past. Anything as 'slow' as dressage frankly bored her, and given the choice her tuition would have concerned jumping and going at speed for ninety per cent of the time.

However, Mrs Hatton-Hall was not making any concessions, and although Anne's class sometimes went out to ride up and down hill to balance horse and rider, and had a fair proportion of instruction in show and cross-country jumping, there were also many hours spent within the confines of the 120 yards × 50 yards covered school. There suppling exercises were the order of the day, army-style drill, plenty of circling at walk, trot and canter, with and without stirrups and work with cavalletti – a series of poles that can be set at different low heights and at varying distances. When the work seemed too slow, Anne sometimes livened up the proceedings and disrupted the class by pinching Jinks behind the saddle to make him buck. She was in her element when it came to equestrian gymnastics like removing one's jacket while taking a jump, or jumping a series of cavalletti without stirrups or reins, with hands on the hips.

She did not always ride Jinks, but at intervals continued to widen her riding education with a variety of the school horses and ponies, quickly growing impatient when she realised it was the quietest that came her way, and triumphant when it was at length conceded she

---

From the start Anne had good balance – and needed it to land safely on occasions like this, when 'all else had failed'! Show-jumping a coloured pony called Slipper in April 1962.

could tackle some of the more awkward customers, including one that skewed sideways as it jumped.

Anne was learning fast, and her first success came in her first summer term, in 1964, during one of the Open Days at Moat House, when she rode as a member of the Benenden School 'A' Team to win the Combined Training Cup. Everyone in this competition had to ride a school animal and Anne's was a co-operative pony called Jester, but she and Jinks were also in the money. They took second place in the individual Junior (fourteen years and under) Combined Training Cup, and a third in the dressage competition for the same age group.

Jinks also profited a great deal from the schooling he was given at Moat House, and from then on Anne's successes began to grow, but it was not until around her last two years with Mrs Hatton-Hall that the penny really dropped on the subject of dressage. Even today it's not her favourite phase of eventing, but she soon realised the difference correct dressage training made to her own pony, and was shrewd enough to aim at the good marks in the dressage test at a Horse Trial, which then gave her more latitude for mistakes in the following cross-country and show-jumping phases. In the Easter, and the summer holidays before going to Balmoral, Anne competed in every Pony Club Horse Trial she could fit in, as well as the occasional gymkhana and hunter trial, and as time went by her name appeared with increasing frequency among the winners.

In October 1968, dressed as a Georgian nobleman, Anne rode a friend's horse as a member of the Battle and District Riding Club team, that competed in the quadrille finals at the Horse of the Year show. And if 'dancing' a quadrille on horseback doesn't come into quite the same category as Combined Training, it would yet be an almost impossible effort for a rider who was not really conversant with dressage training and the correct, imperceptible application of the 'aids'.

The first stages of Anne's competitive riding are alluded to by the

Anne was brought up to study and understand horses and ponies apart from riding them. Here the Queen and her daughter are talking to Benbow, a young horse, originally bred at Sandringham, and brought back there for the Queen to ride in January 1965.

Queen as 'all the nice little days round the golf course jumps', and these years when Anne and Jinks were adding some successes to their increasing pleasure in the sport were for the Queen perhaps the most enjoyable of all. She and her daughter always have the great bond of their mutual interest in horses, but in those stages there was all the fun without any of the pressures. The fences that Anne was tackling with her usual determination and relish bore little resemblance to the apparently terrifying dimensions of those she and Doublet sail over today. The Queen went down to watch the Moat House competitions whenever she could, and sometimes managed to get along to some of the holiday competing as well, and since Anne was still entering 'on the day', these affairs too were relaxed and informal and a lot of fun.

But the years slipped by and in the early spring of 1968, the year Anne was to leave school, Alison Oliver was asked if she would help with the Princess's eventing ambitions, and the first problem was to find a suitable horse. Anne was seventeen, a tall girl who was bent on following through her liking for Junior Eventing into the very different and very tough world of Adult Horse Trials, and a horse of her own, as opposed to a pony, was a necessity. She did not leave school until that July, but before then Jinks was relegated, or promoted, to the role of spoilt, beloved 'family' pony, kept for pleasure riding only.

The transition for any young rider from pony to horse is not altogether easy. It's not purely a question of size – in several, mostly indefinable ways the two have different characteristics, and although Anne was used to riding the royal horses, the bulk of her competing had been in partnership with Jinks. She had however ridden a horse called Blue Star that belonged to the Crown Equerry, in a hunter trial or two, and Colonel Miller suggested to Alison Oliver that this animal might fit the bill. For various reasons that plan fell through, and instead Purple Star was chosen, younger than his brother Blue, and third in the line of the seven bred from the Colonel's former Three Day Event mare, Stella, which he rode in one of the early Olympics.

Purple Star had done a little hunting but was otherwise 'green' and untried, and once again Anne set out to learn the hard way, a novice in adult eventing riding a young, novice horse.

Once more she was lucky. This 15.3 bay gelding that was foaled in

1962 was an ideal character for Anne to take over from a pony. He lacks size for anyone as tall as the Princess to ride at, say, Badminton, but was just right for that stage in her riding career, with a lot of promise and personality, and an innate ability to 'take the mickey' out of anyone at the most inopportune moments which set her the kind of task she relishes, and has never ceased to amuse her.

Alison tried out Purple at a couple of novice events while Anne was in her last Easter term at school, and then in those holidays of early '68 the Princess set about forming a 'Purple' partnership, one that turned out as rewarding as that with Jinks, and was quickly competing with him at Pony Club level. She won the Senior Individual at the South Oxfordshire Pony Club Horse Trials. Most of these try-outs went well, and Anne was really enjoying coping with a little horse that can still play up and buck like a two-year-old if he feels like it. She soon learned never to be too confident with Purple, and even now, when she's got him going beautifully, is never quite certain what he's got up his sleeve. He can be very naughty and takes quite a bit of riding, but he's a very honest horse, gives of his best and is as quick in his jumping as in his thinking, with a cleverness that's pony-like. Purple does not pull, but when he first arrives at a competition he's really quite a handful. He needed, and still needs, riding firmly, particularly in the dressage arena, where any over confidence or relaxing on the part of his rider can result in a sudden, and out of place, scamper to the other side – the kind of joke that Purple obviously finds very funny.

Anne and Purple made their essay into adult events at the end of those Easter holidays, at the Windsor Horse Trials where they combined very well to gain a most satisfactory eighth place. By the time she was next riding him regularly she had left school and life had taken on a new dimension.

In fact Anne left Benenden on July 23rd, and in the following few weeks before she went to Balmoral the new, fully adult status did not quite live up to expectations. This is the moment when the majority of girls are tasting the heady freedom of release from all school restrictions, but Anne left what had been for her the comparative liberty of school to return to the limitations of royal life, which appeared all the more constrictive after acquiring some comparisons with life 'outside'.

Her school friends were all occupied setting about their own independent lives, moving into flats, getting themselves jobs and achieving the measure of freedom that would always be impossible for her. And although social engagements were certainly not lacking and Anne was meeting plenty of people, in these days she knew few of them well enough to look on them as real friends. But Anne, who has inherited the family dislike of wasting time fretting over the unattainable, set out to make the most of something that she could evolve in her own right – her activities with horses.

Although she did not have her own car – a belated eighteenth birthday present – until the October of '68, she had passed her test in the previous April. There were now few days when she was in London or at Windsor, when a borrowed Palace car, Anne at the wheel with her detective beside her, was not heading, fast, for Alison Oliver's stables at Brookfield Farm near Warfield Park – a route the Princess has been taking whenever possible ever since.

There was plenty to do. Riding did not then, and does not now, consist of driving off to some competition with a horse produced and trained by Alison down to the last hair, then climbing on to its back, pressing the right buttons and winning or not according to the luck of the day. Competing with a horse just does not go like that, and even if it did it would never appeal to one of Anne's mentality.

Equally the Princess cannot take on all the schooling of her horses, or the full programme for getting them fit. She is a public figure, for most of the time her riding has to take second place to her public life, and the eventing would be impossible without Alison's help. But as it is a lot of hard work is produced by all concerned, and the results are rewarding – and fun.

If Princess Anne had less ability or been difficult to work with, Alison's job could have been unenviable. Right from the start pupil and instructor got off to a relationship that quickly grew into the kind of uncomplicated, easy friendship that makes everything, from an hour or two's strenuous work in the paddock to a long drive together to a competition, mutually interesting and enjoyable.

Alison Oliver has other pupils beside the Princess and most of these first arrived considerably better equipped than Anne. She gradually

One of the early successes. Princess Anne among the prize-winners at the Eridge Horse Trials in 1969.

acquired what was necessary, and now that she's at the top she has everything she needs in the way of helpful and correct 'tack'. Now there are two dressage saddles and three others for jumping, but she came with very little, and what there was had to be replaced. In the actual riding, her assets were the good balance, and a good seat which only needed slight change, that inborn 'feel' and rhythm to her riding and, as with her mother, the ability to understand and quickly put into practice what is required of her. Also as with the Queen, horses like Anne and go well for her; but although she was so obviously happy and assured on horseback she had little or no technical knowledge, and had never had the opportunity of studying the training and schooling of a horse, or of applying this important side of riding for herself.

One of the essentials of competitive riding is the right outlook in the competitor, and here Anne is lucky to have inherited her father's tremendous determination and ability to rise to the occasion. She is never ruthless with her horses, yet enters every Horse Trial all out to win. If things go wrong she is very honest in assessing the causes, is annoyed if it's her own fault, and does not easily forgive herself her own mistakes, although her horse's are a different matter.

The set-up at Brookfield helped Anne acquire her philosophical approach to the uncertain fortunes of eventing. There were plenty of other people, coming and going to competitions, with horses that had gone splendidly last time out, and then inexplicably decided to have an off day, and this helped her to get the right assessment, the right approach to life with horses. She still gets angry with herself, the language can flow if she comes a cropper or someone gets in the way, but when things don't go according to plan she can shrug it off as just 'one of those things . . .' or, quoting back at her instructor, tongue in cheek, remark, 'Oh, well, it's all good experience!'

There was still a long way to go, but by the autumn of 1968 Anne and Purple were competing in most of the Novice Horse Trials and being consistently placed.

Maybe some of Doublet's proved stamina traces back through his Argentine ancestry to the feral mustangs that roamed America. His mother, Suerte, seen here the year after Doublet was born and grazing at Sandringham with the Queen Mother's Honeypot Lane, was one of Prince Philip's first Argentine polo ponies.

CHAPTER FIVE

Enter Doublet

PRINCE Philip's enthusiasm for polo, fostered by his uncle, Earl Mountbatten, began in Malta while he was still serving with the Royal Navy. His liking for the game, and his skill, quickly increased, and he soon acquired ponies of his own back at home. One of the first of these was a liver chestnut Argentine mare, with two white socks and a white star, called Suerte.

Argentine polo ponies are descended from the Criollo cow ponies, first used for polo in South America, that since the beginning of the century have been specially bred up for the game with imported, top-class Thoroughbred stock, until they are now virtually an accepted

polo breed. Nowadays these ponies, considered by the majority of high-goal players to be the finest for polo in the world, themselves much resemble Thoroughbreds but are slightly smaller, tougher and have less excitable temperaments.

Criollos owe the fantastic endurance for which they are famed to their Mustang forebears, those 'wild' descendants of the Conquistadors' Spanish mounts that escaped to form great herds of feral horses roaming the New World. Through succeeding generations these Mustangs lost some of their original elegance, but acquired instead exceptional stamina and intelligence – characteristics much appreciated by the early American settlers who caught and used them as cow ponies. In North America the Mustang strain is now almost entirely bred out, but in the South it is retained to a great extent in the various forms of Criollo. Suerte and her offspring reflect her tough ancestry.

As with many of Prince Philip's favourite pony mares, when Suerte was retired from polo she was sent to Sandringham as a brood mare. She bred a number of polo ponies and some riding horses – the latter usually those that through the lush grazing and good care of the stud at Sandringham have grown too big for polo. One of her daughters, a handsome chestnut named Effingham, went to Windsor as a riding horse for the Queen. In 1963 Suerte produced a colt foal by Doubtless, an Argentine-bred Thoroughbred that had raced in Britain.

The colt, a chestnut like its mother, was strong and lively, and even as a handsome yearling was obviously, like his full sister Effingham, going to be too big for polo. As with all the stud foals, the chestnut had been halter-broken and well handled from birth, and any tendency to cheekiness firmly checked, but when, by then named Doublet, he was of an age for breaking-in and first training, Suerte's son was not one of the easier propositions. He settled down however, although his future still remained uncertain. Then, when he was nearly six, approaching 16.2 hands and showing a potential that seemed worth exploring, it was decided to send Doublet to Alison Oliver as a possible Eventer for Princess Anne.

Almost from the first moment she clapped eyes on him, Alison felt there was something a bit 'special' about Doublet, a hunch that grew stronger the more she rode him. It was obvious that he was still

Bussaco, the Portuguese Lusitano stallion, exercising in the indoor school at Windsor in 1964. Exceptionally amiable and highly schooled, he was frequently used for riding by the Queen's guests, but before being loaned to a stud, where he was eventually put down in 1969, Bussaco fathered the foal, Oporto, with which Princess Anne is conversing on this book-jacket.

Doublet (*left*) as a yearling, in 1964. In those days, to Princess Anne, he was just one of the young stock always to be seen grazing the sheltered paddocks at Sandringham, but the Queen would have known his parentage at a glance – and had probably already decided that here was another handsome youngster growing much too big for polo!

straightening out from being rather a difficult young horse and he proved sensitive and individualistic, needing a lot of understanding, but he rapidly grew more reliable. She was certain the horse had a lot of ability. She also felt that Doublet was just the animal for Princess Anne to take on at that stage, being both demanding and rewarding.

Anne herself was not so sure. By then she had acquired another horse, Royal Ocean, and was fully occupied schooling and eventing him and Purple. The two could scarcely be less alike, little Purple Star

with his liveliness and naughtiness and ability to rise to the occasion, and Ocean, a big, long striding reliable Thoroughbred, by a French horse called Garçon, that had raced in his youth and was very fast – a horse that did his job well but just lacked the personality and 'spark' of Purple.

Anne was having fun with these two, but the original schooling sessions with Doublet did not prove a great success. Somehow she could not combine with this horse, and there was a stage quite early on when she felt she never would. Anne has, however, complete faith in her trainer's judgement. If Alison thought the world of Doublet and was convinced he had great scope, then obviously the fault lay with Anne's own handling of the situation. Here was a new challenge to take up, and she accepted it with her usual keenness.

Soon, as the training progressed and the weeks went by Anne and Doublet began to understand each other, and started to form the relationship of mutual trust and confidence between rider and horse that is one of the most rewarding aspects of riding, and without which success in any form of equestrian competing is unlikely.

In the meantime the competing, still at novice standard, with the other two was going well. A try-out at a Horse Trial at Liphook on April 2nd was satisfactory, but without producing a place. Five days later Anne took both horses to the Taplow Horse Show, in Buckinghamshire, for a go at the Foxhunter Show-Jumping class, and, after two clears in the first round, ended up with an equal fourth with Purple. On the 10th she was at Everdon for another Trial but luck was not on her side that day. A good dressage score and a clear in the show-jumping phase gave her the lead with both horses, but trouble at the same fence on the cross-country in each case put paid to their hopes. With both of them Anne was clear so far, but number 14, a tricky 5-feet drop into the farmyard took Purple by surprise and he stopped, while Ocean, with Anne quite resolved not to risk a refusal with him

---

above: Even way back in '69 some of the fences looked quite formidable. The Princess taking Royal Ocean over a spread in the Windsor Park Horse Trials.

below: Princess Anne found Purple Star just the right companion for partnering her earlier ventures in the world of adult eventing.

also, was pushed on into it so firmly that he met it wrong and fell. No luck that day, but some very valuable experience.

The remainder of April produced a fourth for jumping at Newbury, followed by a rewarding day out at Stokenchurch – when Anne collected a first and a second for the Novice Class in a Combined Competition – which consists of a dressage test of Preliminary or Novice Standard, and a course of fences not exceeding 3 feet 9 inches in height or 5 feet in spread.

Purple Star was now qualified for Intermediate Classes, and was to compete in one at the Windsor Horse Trials on April 30th, but in the event only Ocean was able to go as Purple had by then started coughing, a victim to the infectious ailment that is one of the bugbears of the game and can put a horse off work for weeks.

There were 102 horses for the four Novice Sections of the Trials, with twenty-seven starters in Princess Anne's Section D. She and Ocean put on an excellent dressage test for seventeen penalty points, were unpenalised in the show jumping and went clear across country with seven time faults to give them a convincing win – eight points ahead of Mark Phillips on Great Ovation, who were to be the winners at Badminton in 1971.

Public interest in Princess Anne's eventing was getting beyond the stage when any successes excited journalists only because she was who she was. The national press were still not always entirely clear as to the nature of her particular sport – only after Burghley did headlines such as 'ANOTHER SHOW-JUMPING SUCCESS FOR ANNE' really become a thing of the past – but surmises were beginning to circulate that, at the time, seemed fairly wild and exaggerated. Alison Oliver was plainly delighted with her pupil's progress, quickness at assimilating what was required and with her natural aptitude and competitive spirit, but she was still only competing at novice level, and to start talking about her going to the very top, not to mention riding in the Olympics, seemed ridiculously premature and out of place.

One outcome of that season of 1969 that meant a great deal to Anne was that long before it was over she had been accepted by the eventing world as one of themselves, judged on performance and liked for herself – none the less for the quick temper and blistering tongue that can occasionally sear those who distract her horse from the job in hand, and particularly for her ready laughter and tremendous sense of humour.

In the family circle Anne had her mother's one hundred per cent interest. The Queen's professed hobby is horses, in its widest sense –

Like the Queen, Princess Anne has a *rapport* with all horses and ponies. When she catches up the riding animals at Balmoral this little Fell pony, Tinker, is usually included for one of the younger children to ride.

one that she confesses she has never outgrown and which certainly does not just concern racehorses but all types of 'the animal on four legs'. She still contrived to follow her daughter's fortunes without attracting the over-publicity that could have made the competing more difficult for Anne. Both the Queen and the Princess, one to watch and one to compete, managed to arrive at Taplow with only the show officials in the know about their coming. On the home ground at Windsor both the Queen and Prince Philip were able to spend an informal day enjoying the highlights of the Trial, and sharing Anne's delight at winning.

On June 26th that year there was an added edge to their interest. Anne rode Doublet to win a Dressage Competition at Basingstoke, in public together for the first time – and notched up a second on Royal Ocean for good measure. This was an exciting outing – a win in the form of competing for which Anne once had no use, when riding the horse, first time out, with which she once couldn't combine. For the Queen there was the extra enjoyment of it being her own animal, the horse she had bred – even if he was intended to be a polo pony – and for Prince Philip it was a triumph for his favourite Suerte's offspring.

Only a month later Anne won the Novice Class at Osberton, Doublet's first complete Horse Trial. Again they knocked up an excellent dressage score, the best overall in the novice sections; had one fence down in the show-jumping, but then went clear, with two time faults, in the cross-country, ending up with a total of thirty penalty points – and a resultant qualification for Doublet for the Midland Bank Novice Championships at Chatsworth, to finish the season on October 18th.

In between those dates very satisfactory placings, a third and two seconds in Trials at Eridge, Powderham Castle in Devon, and Stoneleigh Abbey, kept the good work going, with a second in the Intermediate Class at Wylye and and eleventh at Stokenchurch and an eighth at Tweseldown as the lowest on the list. It must have been a very pleasing end to an encouraging year of competing, to collect a well-earned sixth, with such a relatively inexperienced performer as Doublet, in the Chatsworth Championships.

With much the same competitive spirit and outlook as Anne, Prince Philip couldn't fail to understand her love of this sport, and was as proud as any other father of his daughter's achievements, but both he and the Queen felt it might be a good thing if Anne could find another enthusiasm as well as horses. Prince Philip considers that all young people should try for some kind of demonstrable achievement in their life that they can look back on. At that time it seemed to him a far-off chance that Anne would ever hit the international level in riding, and even if she did he doubted whether it would last her for always as an ultimate, substantial accomplishment. Yet Badminton and Burghley in '71 obviously delighted him and fostered his pride in his daughter's ability.

It's a great relief to the royal family to have someone with the unruffled competence of Alison Oliver to help with, and keep an eye on Anne's riding programme. The Queen doesn't fuss about her family's sporting activities – as she says, one *can* break a leg falling out of bed; but, as to any other parent, those fences at Badminton somehow tend to loom even larger when it's her own daughter who is tackling them, and it's a comfort at such times to know that the trainer concerned is both determined and careful. Alison doesn't fuss either, and it's a combination of working with someone who has this trait allied to the Princess's own innate 'cool',. that enables Anne to cope calmly with the various inevitable vicissitudes attached to eventing. And it's necessary to be able to keep one's head on occasions like that at the Stokenchurch Horse Trials in 1971, when one of Anne's young grey horses made a mistake and straddled the first part of a double, rustic parallel bars set above a typical little beechwood coombe with another pair at the bottom. The next few seconds must have seemed a long time, and there was only the fence judge, a lady, in sight to help at need, but Anne sat still and talked to her horse, until he managed somehow to scramble off and they could have another, more successful, go.

CHAPTER SIX

Home and abroad

THE ability to remain calm and appear unruffled also stood Anne in good stead when she first began on the round of her own public duties, early in 1969. She was only eighteen, and although she had attended a number of public ceremonies with the Queen and Prince Philip, it was a different matter being out on her own. In this context also, however, she proved good at rising to the occasion, but it must have been helpful that one of the earliest engagements concerned her own particular hobby, and that one way and another, and not always of intent, there's an occasional flavour of horse interest spicing some of her public life.

After going round the Rover Works at Solihull on April 25th, 1969 – and since Anne is mechanically minded, that was another particularly interesting engagement – she went on to take a look at the National Equestrian Centre near Kenilworth.

This is the equivalent of an equestrian 'university', and the Princess found a lot to catch her attention in the office block, concerned with all the administration of the different branches of horse lore connected with the British Horse Society. She was able to inspect the registration of her own Purple Star, and then went to see the other facilities that include a big indoor riding school.

There were various aspects of the day to day activities at the Centre to watch, a horse being lunged, another being schooled, and then a riding class for spastic and disabled children. The Princess was impressed by the unmistakable bliss of the handicapped riders, and amused at the miscellany of shapes and sizes of pony taking part, the one essential for this work being a really quiet and co-operative temperament. In 1971 Princess Anne was to remember this scene, when she agreed to become patron to the Riding for the Disabled Association, giving active support to a scheme that does wonderful physically and mentally therapeutic work for the less fortunate. In May 1972 she was present at a display given by disabled riders at Crabbet Park.

Sometimes there's the obvious equine link in Princess Anne's engagements. Occasions such as the evening, before she went on to receive the trophy voted her by the British Sports Writers' Association,

Princess Anne at the Royal Army Veterinary Corps Training Centre, Melton Mowbray, in March 1972. Seen here in company with Gamekeeper, an eight-year-old ridden by the Mexico Olympic Gold Medallist, Staff. Serg. Ben Jones.

when she was admitted as an Honorary Freeman of the Worshipful Company of Farriers, and attended their dinner. And since the old saying 'no foot, no horse' is as true as ever it was, and this ancient Livery Company of London ensures the standard of those increasingly rare jewels, the skilled Shoeing Smiths, by granting them proficiency certificates after a rigorous examination, that was an evening that concerned all horsemen.

Two years earlier the intrusion of a horse into a ceremony held at Paderborn in Germany was not quite as intended. The animal in question, borrowed from another regiment as a mount for an orderly escort, was enhancing the ceremonial parade put on by the 14th/20th King's Hussars for Princess Anne when she visited them in the capacity of their recently appointed Colonel-in-Chief. In theory the horse's role was a purely static one, positioned behind the saluting base where the Princess stood, but after the unrehearsed descent of the royal standard down the flag-pole just beside it, the animal's by then shattered nerve broke when a horde of photographers surged towards the saluting base – and it took off complete with orderly for an unsignified destination.

Official duties concerning agricultural shows and their like obviously bring a quota of watching horses, shown in hand, under saddle, jumping or driven. The 1969 Bath and West Show at Shepton Mallet provided also a bonus – the exhilarating musical ride put on by the contingent of the Royal Canadian Mounted Police that was touring Britain that year, and the chance afterwards of a stroll between the horse-lines to meet the performers, both two-legged and four.

For some years the Princess has been accompanying the Queen and Prince Philip to some of the big sporting events like the Derby, and she was with them when they were guests of the Australian Jockey Club, to watch the racing at Randwick, Sydney, on April 1st, 1970, and again three days later at Mowbray in Tasmania, but it's no good pretending Anne particularly relishes the role of onlooker. Like her father she's by nature a 'doer'. She enjoys the annual houseparty at Windsor for

---

above: Derby Day 1969. The Queen and the Queen Mother watch with Princess Anne as the runners canter down to the start. The Princess is sometimes one of the Royal party on big sporting occasions, but she much prefers being a participant in riding sports to taking the static role of spectator!

below: During Royal Ascot Week the Princess's chief enjoyment is the 'family' scamper up the course in the early hours, that was started by the Queen when she was a girl. Here is Anne leading the Royal field in 1970, and as happens nowadays, showing them a clean pair of heels!

17
18

left:
The show-jumping phase at Chatsworth gives Anne and Doublet a chance to prove their versatility over painted fences.

above:
This occasion in Hong Kong gave Anne the opportunity to ride over and peep across to China.

Ascot week, but for her the highlight is neither the authentic racing nor the traditional 'fashion show' in the paddock – but that impromptu 'royal' race up the course in the early morning, inaugurated by the Queen as a girl, when Anne and some chosen eventing companion give the other riders a good start, and then indulge in a real lickety-split gallop.

One guerdon that Anne receives through her well-publicised hobby is the chance to ride different types of horses on some of her official tours abroad, the animals produced either as part of the schedule, or as a well deserved means of relaxation.

In May 1969 a bout of flu prevented Anne accompanying the Queen and Prince Philip on the first two days of their state visit to Austria. She missed some of the magnificent ceremonies, including the spectacular display specially put on by the riders and horses of the famous Spanish Riding School in Vienna, but she was in time for other festivities, and to visit the state stud where the Lipizzaners for the school are bred. There she was able to see the young stock, and the mares with their foals – which are born dark brown and do not change colour for four years or longer – grazing the health-giving mountain pastures at Piber, where the stud was installed after the last war through the understanding and co-operation of the American Army.

Back again in Vienna, Anne was able to watch a practice ride in the school, and then had the fascinating opportunity to ride one of the horses for herself.

These are all white Lipizzaner stallions, descendants of the noble Spanish horses that can be traced back to the time of Caesar, and that were imported by the Archduke Charles of Inner Austria in 1580 to form a stud in the village of Lipizza, near Trieste. The splendid horses of today are the result of centuries of breeding from Spanish, Italian and Arabic-Oriental blood, and in conformation, stamina, intelligence and temperament are exactly suited for work in the riding academy where classical horsemanship is still cultivated in its purest form. Some of the manoeuvres are based on medieval cavalry tactics, others have their roots in the natural curvets of young horses at play or of stallions fighting, but, although these Lipizzaners are particularly adapted to the arts they are required to perform, they do not do them on their own.

It requires years of the most careful schooling of both the horse and its eventual trainer to achieve the standards demanded for any of the beautifully controlled movements used in the Spanish Riding School – not to mention the 'airs above the ground', such as the rear up and jump forward called the courbette; the levade, when the horse sits back motionless on its haunches with forehand raised; or the incredible leap off through the air, with hind legs outstretched, that is the capriole.

No rider who has not made a special study of *haute école* could produce even a modest show with one of these Lipizzaners, and there are many, very good horsemen by other standards, who could so muddle a trained Spanish School horse by using the aids incorrectly or indecisively, that the animal might be too confused even to move.

All the stallions belong to one of the six original lines, and Princess Anne rode the thirteen-year-old Siglavy Bona, that traces back to the Arab 'Siglavy'. The animal had never before been ridden by a woman, and it says much for the Princess's good tuition through the years, real

Riding Siglavy Bona in the Spanish Riding School at Vienna in 1969.

above left: Family riding at Sandringham in 1965. Anne had to lead Andrew from Benbow because the Queen's horse Betsy sometimes took exception to the Shetland Valkyrie.

below left: King George V planted this avenue of trees at Sandringham and left an extra wide verge beside the road with horsemen in mind. The Queen and Princess Anne enjoying a canter.

above right: Anne with the Queen's young horse Benbow outside Sandringham House. He was bred on the estate.

grasp of dressage and ability to put into effect what she is being told, that Bona co-operated with her so willingly. She was instructed by Colonel Johann Handler, Head of the Spanish School, and after a while managed to get the correct timing to achieve creditable 'flying changes' – when the horse changes its feet in mid-air so that the 'inside' legs are leading as it canters circles, either to left or right. She went on to other of the more simple movements, including a passage, and then to the difficult 'piaffe' – a lofty trot performed without moving forward, which Anne thought very remarkable and satisfying . . . provided one can get it right!

While she was in Austria Anne also had her first meeting with the pair of native Haflinger pony mares, an attractive sturdy mountain breed, which were presented to the Queen and which Anne drove in public a short while afterwards. Back home the ponies were sent to Balmoral, where they were trained for stalking and to go in double harness.

The Queen learned to drive during the early part of World War II, when she and Princess Margaret were in Scotland and used their ponies for transport, either riding or driving. She competed in, and won, a Driving Class at the Royal Windsor Show in 1940, and when Andrew was a baby the Queen was lent a pair of New Forest ponies which she drove occasionally at Windsor. More recently, Prince Philip has become increasingly interested in the art of driving, and in 1971 was one of the chief instigators of a driving competition that he attended in Hungary. It's therefore not surprising that Princess Anne should know something of the art too, and she agreed to become the thousandth member of the British Driving Society – even though she really prefers having a little more actual contact with her horse, as obtained in riding, than that possible with the more remote control in driving.

The Haflingers were only six years old but like all of their breed well used to drawing sleighs and the more utilitarian sledges up and down the Austrian mountains in winter, but Anne only had two ten-minute practice sessions with them before embarking, with her youngest brother Edward as passenger, on a meeting of the British Driving Society held on Smith's Lawn in June '69.

Although the Haflingers were obviously well used to harness work, it was the first time they had encountered numbers of people and a public occasion like this, and as Anne 'bent' them in and out of the horse-lines on her way to the ring, she was impressed with their good behaviour – and thankful too, as she felt she might very easily have been out of control without the ponies' willing assistance! They also behaved admirably in their class, the Concours d'Élegance, and the royal entourage added to the very attractive sight of seventy-five vehicles of different types, all trotting round the perimeter. The Princess was driving her ponies to the French Chaise – the carriage that Edward VII, as Prince of Wales, gave to his Princess in 1875, and with which the Queen, then Princess Elizabeth, won at Windsor with a Fell pony.

Unlike her mother, Anne did not win – her carriage and pair were much admired, but the Haflingers were thought by some to be a little big for the Chaise – but she was judged as one of the rightful runners-up for the Carriage Cup.

Accompanying the Queen and Prince Philip on their Commonwealth Tour in the spring of 1970 provided no opportunities for driving, and not much time for riding. However, two horses were provided in New Zealand, and Anne had an unexpectedly hilarious ride in South Island. There was also a hack for her to try early on in Australia almost as soon as she landed. And after a daily succession of public engagements, with her parents and on her own, in Sydney, Hobart, Launceston, Melbourne, Timbertop with Prince Charles, Port Kembla, Newcastle, Broadmeadow, Coffs Harbour and Brisbane, before continuing with the round Anne flew off on a two day visit to a private property, 'Talbarea' Station at Cunnamulla – where she met up with that indispensable and admirable Australian institution, the station horse.

Twice since the original showing in 1971, devotees of the BBC children's programme *Blue Peter* have been able to watch the film that was made on Princess Anne's visit to Kenya. And as well as admiring Anne's extensive knowledge of the Starehe Boys' Centre – as president of the Save the Children Fund this big overseas project was the Princess's chief objective – they were able to watch her in a riding session, filmed with *Blue Peter*'s Val Singleton. They rode together through a coffee plantation, Anne wearing blue jeans and a patterned

Anne shares her parents' interest in driving. With Edward as passenger she exhibited the Queen's Haflinger ponies from Austria in the British Driving Society's Windsor meeting.

Different terrain and different scenery – not to mention different horses – all go towards furthering Anne's enjoyment of riding.

shirt, her horse, Silver Tip, a flea-bitten grey polo pony of typical African, Arab-cum-Barb, breeding.

The sequence included Anne talking about her ambitions as a three-day event rider and explaining the nature of the sport, but one incident

– only shown on television when the Princess was in the studios back home, displaying her photographs of Kenyan wild life prior to the actual film – was quite unpremeditated. Talking finished, Anne had been, as always, ready to comply with a request for a bit of speed, but as the riders came round a grove of eucalyptus trees at the gallop, an unexpected encounter with a tractor sent Val Singleton's animal off at a tangent, with a series of bucks that culminated in a nasty fall.

No such contretemps accompanied Princess Anne's riding at the Imperial Stud outside Tehran, when she and Prince Philip were in Iran in 1971 representing the Queen at the magnificent celebrations, staged at Persepolis, of that ancient country's 2,500 years of history. The stables are at Farahabad outside Tehran, the small 'rest' Palace, extensive stabling and sanded exercise paddock with its collection of made-up jumps, all dominated by the rocky heights of the Elburz mountains, the glistening snow-capped cone of Demavend rising over all.

The Shah is a fine horseman, and although nowadays he has little time for indulging his favourite form of exercise Farahabad and the Master of the Horse, Captain Cambyses Atabai, have a great deal to do with the newly formed Royal Horse Society of Iran, and the awakened interest in equine sports that is rapidly growing in parts of the country. Prince Philip and Anne were very interested to learn of all that is going on and to see for themselves the different types of horses that are bred at the stud. They inspected the Shah's favourite riding stallions, among them Turkomans from the arid steppeland south-east of the Caspian, Persian Plateau horses bred by the tribes that wander the central plateau and slopes of the Zagros mountains, Darashouli from the deserts of the South, all trained to stand motionless until the Shah is mounted, and then to exhibit the speed that he enjoys.

The Princess rode one of these, a three-year-old stallion called Belderchine, using one of the fine saddles of French make with which the stud is well equipped. The horse is part Thoroughbred-Persian-Plateau-Arab, with the fiery yet obedient nature that is characteristic of Persian horses, and the cat-like surefootedness that the terrain demands. Like all Middle-Eastern breeds, Belderchine has the greyhound conformation of the desert horse, and Anne remarked on how narrow he

---

When Princess Anne goes abroad on official visits, a horse of some kind or another usually figures in the programme somewhere. When she was in Kenya in February 1971, as President of the Save the Children Fund her chief objective was the Starehe Boys' Centre in Nairobi, but there were other interesting side-lines as well. A BBC camera team were filming the Royal 'safari' for their programme *Blue Peter*, and included a riding session. The Princess was loaned a grey polo-pony called Silver Tip, and as always, both before and after riding, quickly got on good terms with her mount.

seemed after those to which she is accustomed. But her horsemanship is now such that she completely adapted to her mount within a few moments, and found him an excellent and enjoyable ride. Accompanied by the British Military Attaché and Mrs Firouz, who has a stud of the miniature 'Caspian horses' outside Tehran, she set off on a ten-mile ride up into the Imperial hunting reserves.

They rode into the foothills, on a sandy track through the young plantations close by the stud that changes after a while to a clamber over bare rock, with unexpected fissures, loose shale and stone, on up past tamarisk bushes and the occasional acacia tree. They rode the narrow trails made by muflon – the wild sheep that inhabit the region in their thousands and that are stalked with rifles – glimpsed a herd running on the mountainside, saw partridge and blue pigeon and a hawk hanging motionless above. The trails cross the occasional stream, where the damp ground may hold the pad-mark of a wolf, or wind through gorges where leopards sometimes lurk among the overhanging rocks, and to Anne it was all a new and exciting adventure. But it was when they turned for home, and came off the mountains and headed for the stud at the gallop, in a wide, five-mile sweep across to the east of Tehran, that she knew the exhilaration of a pace she loves, with a type of horse renowned for speed.

The Iranians are well known as individualists who recognise a man's worth and give him credit for it, and they are also great sportsmen. Princess Anne's horsemanship did not go unremarked that day; her handling of Belderchine was thought very impressive, and Captain Atabai was all the more pleased to present to her, on behalf of the Shah, a beautiful bay colt called Atesh, which means fire. It is a Pahlavan, a new breed named for the dynasty that is being developed at the stud from Thoroughbred, Persian Plateau and Jadran Arab, in

With Val Singleton, of the *Blue Peter* programme, Princess Anne had an enjoyable ride through groves of eucalyptus trees, beside a river and on the fringe of huge coffee plantations. They rode into an African village where the children crowded out to talk to them without any idea that one of the riders was Princess Anne, and where one of the boys proudly produced a tiny, new-born puppy for her inspection.

the proportions of 50:25:25, with both speed and endurance as characteristics.

Because of African Horse Sickness it was not immediately possible to bring Atesh into England, but it is hoped that eventually a way can be found that is consistent with quarantine regulations.

Any chance that Anne gets to ride an alien type of horse in a new environment adds to her riding experience as well as being very enjoyable. She now has a proven ability to adjust quickly to different animals, and this has greatly contributed to the speed with which she has been able to upgrade such dissimilar types as Purple Star, Royal Ocean, and Doublet, and now Columbus and Collingwood.

Princess Anne at Farahabad, the Imperial Stud in Iran, during her visit to that country with Prince Philip for the 2,500th anniversary celebrations of the Persian Empire. She is riding Belderchine, one of the Shahanshah's favourite stallions, that like most of his kind combines a fiery disposition with obedience, and the Princess found him a delightful ride.

CHAPTER SEVEN

Training – and Badminton 1971

NOWADAYS a points system is used for upgrading horses, but before 1972 it was done on winnings. And since eventing, particularly at the lower levels, does not produce vast sums as prize-money it was not all that easy to pick up the £15 necessary to leave novice status, let alone the £40 that upgraded to Open or Advanced.

Purple Star became an Intermediate horse in the autumn of '69, and a good win at Liphook a year later put him into Open events. Doublet

upgraded to Intermediate in the autumn of his first eventing year, also in 1969, and followed suit with Purple to become an Open horse the following year. But by this time Royal Ocean's competing days were over.

In the previous October, and for the first time, Anne had cut short her family holiday at Balmoral, and returned south to fit in some intensive riding and as many competitions as she could. Among other fixtures she rode Ocean in the Spiller's Combined Competition at the Horse of the Year Show at Wembley Stadium, but was unplaced. She was show jumping at Tweseldown on the 12th, and a week later took Ocean and Doublet to Chatsworth.

This was for the Novice Horse Trials Championships where she and Doublet were to score a sixth place, but before embarking on the clear across country with her chestnut horse, Anne had the unfamiliar and worrying experience of Ocean refusing at three different jumps. With such a reliable animal it was obvious all was not well, and she wisely retired. Eventually, after a lot of investigation and thought it was decided Ocean's retirement should be permanent, and he is ending his days happily at Windsor in the role of royal riding horse.

Many event horses and riders come to eventing after an initiation in the rough and tumble of the hunting field, where they gain invaluable experience of jumping different obstacles under all kinds of conditions and going. For various reasons this was not possible for Princess Anne, and although Purple had seen hounds about twice before she had him, and Ocean had done a little racing, they were both complete novices to the sport, while Doublet and the Queen's young horses that the Princess now rides as well, came straight to Brookfield Farm after their breaking-in. And since Anne herself was also a novice to adult eventing and all that it entails, the speed with which she has upgraded her 'string' is, at least, out of the ordinary.

Perhaps there has been an element of luck in obtaining untried, home-bred horses of such potential, but basically it has come about

---

previous page: Jumping Purple, Anne demonstrates her excellent seat – sensitive hands giving the horse all the rein he needs, weight off his loins, the rider in rhythm and balance with her horse.

through happy and eminently fruitful teamwork. Anne contributes above-average riding ability, and the dedicated will to ride well, and win. And although in many respects, and contrary to some public belief, in the context of this sport her background is more hindrance than help, she has in fact been brought up to give of her best whatever she may be doing, whether it's appearing in public to launch a ship or riding at a fence.

On Alison's side is her gift for putting over, both to a rider and to a horse, exactly what is required, her meticulous eye for spotting what is wrong, and her endless patience in getting it right. She is expert at the intricate art of feeding horses and getting them fit as individuals, and she's there to carry on with the horses and their training when the Princess, owing to public commitments, is not. The horses themselves form the base of this triangular partnership, and the uncomplicated, unpretentious and relaxed atmosphere at Brookfield is a big contributory factor to the overall success.

There's nothing remotely resembling the smart 'school of equitation' type of place about the two rows, facing each other, of very 'homey' loose-boxes, with room for twenty-six horses in all. An empty haynet or two hang on nails beside open doorways, rugs are slung on

Alison Oliver, wife of the well-known show-jumper Alan Oliver, who formed the successful training 'partnership' with Princess Anne and her eventing horses in 1968. Alison has herself been 'in the running' for selection in an Olympic eventing team, learned dressage from a world expert, and is skilled at extracting the best from riders and horses in her care.

the half-doors to air, skeps, a stable broom, a fork, a barrow of droppings are in evidence, a couple of headcollars lying outside their owners' empty boxes, all giving an air, not of untidiness but of an essentially working ménage, where the precise orderliness of a place 'on show' would be totally inappropriate. A horse is being led out for a bite of grass, another comes in from lungeing, a chestnut gelding stands in the sun to be sponged down after exercise by its owner-pupil, a girl groom is bridling Purple, another mucking out Doublet's box. None of them stops what he or she is doing, but greets Anne with the same friendly ease she displays towards them – someone who belongs around the place.

The facilities match the rest of it. There's no elaborate cross-country course for training. On the rough patch of grass between the stables and the galvanised iron side of the indoor school, a few obstacles have been constructed – a big, sleeper-faced bank with a smaller one beside it; an open ditch, another with a diagonal rail over it, a couple of fences up between the trees at the back of the school.

left: Good jumping is an essential for success in eventing, but most of the schooling takes place 'on the ground'. Here Doublet is being worked so that he becomes both active and relaxed.

above: Schooling is a relaxed affair down at Brookfield Farm. Though its purpose is serious, it is enjoyed by both Anne and Doublet.

Anne leaves nothing to chance. Like every top-notch competitor she knows that walking the course beforehand, in the way you mean to ride it, is essential for success. The inevitable attentions of the Press can be a problem, but an amicable compromise on the big occasions provides for mass photography at a fence or two – then Anne is left in peace to study the best approaches and pick out the most workable route. Strict attention to every detail can lead to success – and the smile of a winner!

The small home paddock is fenced with wooden railings, with two or three places built up for jumping in and out. And when Anne goes off with one of her horses on to the road, to ride up by herself the half mile or so to the jumping field, it's the same story up there. No elaborate set of show fences, but half a dozen painted jumps, with sufficient poles and wings and bits and pieces for Alison, now following to the field by car, to arrange into different combinations.

Out in the middle of this big field is a complex of posts and rails – a cross-country fence of the sort that can be jumped in different ways and from different angles, on the principle of the 'Cat's Cradle' at Badminton. Round the perimeter of the field, where a couple of girls may be galloping their own horses while the jumping goes on, are a rustic wall and two or three other cross-country jumps.

Schooling and practising the dressage movements take place on the soft tan and wood-shaving floor of the indoor school, which boasts a couple of mirrors for riders to judge how it's going, and where the walls are marked off at the correct intervals with the alphabetical letters used in a dressage arena. Riders and horses take their fitness exercise out and around Warfield Park and the surrounding countryside, and gain their experience by competing.

By 1970 all this was a very familiar and happy part of Anne's life. Her public duties were a first priority, her riding a deep interest that was fitted in around them – and those who occasionally clamour for the Princess to be 'allowed' to do nothing but the riding she so obviously enjoys know little of her character and of the inherited and deep-seated sense of duty that motivates her outlook. When she's in London it's routine to be up by 7.30 am or before, so that there can be a dash down to Brookfield for two or three hours' schooling, but then it's back for whatever engagement is fixed for the day. When she's at Windsor there's a ride in the Park with Jinks or one of the other riding horses at 8 am and then an evening session with Alison Oliver if it can be fitted in. For the past year or so the Princess's diary of engagements has been arranged to try and give her a little more time to prepare for the big eventing occasion such as Badminton. Before the '71 Badminton she managed to fit in helpful 'specialist' competitions, concentrating on different phases – in March she had both Doublet and Purple in the Novice Dressage Championships at Stoneleigh, and gained a second and a fourth respectively, followed by a fourth with Doublet in the Medium Class. She took them both to compete, successfully, in an indoor jumping show at Wing and was eventing at Kinlet on April 10th, but there's no opting out of prearranged public duties in favour of some tempting competition.

In 1972 while all the top-notch riders were stepping up their training and fitness programmes in preparation for Badminton and possible selection to train on for Munich, Princess Anne was on a royal tour of Asia with the Queen and Prince Philip. In those weeks while she was away Alison could continue with Doublet's preparation, but she

couldn't supply the other elements essential to success – the rider's training and physical fitness, the everyday work-out together of rider and horse that spells mutual confidence and welds them into a team. Anne flew into Heathrow Airport from Singapore on the evening of March 5th and was out working Doublet as usual the next morning. There were only thirty-one days to go to Badminton; not all of those could be utilised, and it meant what it usually does only more so – lots and lots of the highly concentrated strenuous hard work, on which Anne thrives . . . even if she does confess to being lazy by nature!

All through the 1970 season the good work went on with Doublet and Purple. Sometimes the flavour of the outings was altered a little, like the good school both horses were given over coloured jumps in the Foxhunter Class at Aldershot on June 5th. Time faults robbed Anne of a first, but she got a second with Purple and a third with Doublet, and had the satisfaction of riding three clear rounds with each horse – which involved jumping sixty fences without a fault.

Usually the days went well – by then both horses could be depended on more frequently than not to pull something out of the bag – but sometimes they didn't, and Anne met up with the usual mixture of good and bad luck, and the occasional mishaps and mistakes that are the lot of every rider. She had a fall or two – between the spring of '68 and that of '72 her total quota was around six, at least in public. She has been winded and temporarily dazed, but happily not otherwise injured since cracking a little finger way back in 1964, and breaking her nose a few years later.

When she brought both horses into Kent in September 1970 for a one-day Horse Trial at Knowlton Court, near Canterbury, Purple did a good dressage for 28 penalty points, followed up with a clear in the show-jumping, but then collected a 20 on the cross-country. Doublet's dressage was not as good, by 7 penalties, and he played around in the show-jumping to clock up a further 11, only to sail gaily across country without a fault. Neither were in the money – Doublet scored a total of 46 to make him seventh, Purple finished up with a 48 –

---

previous pages: A horse quickly becomes put off if asked to jump too many big fences and in training Anne aims for accuracy in approach and take-off and leaves the more formidable obstacles for competition.

However fit you are, and Princess Anne shows sense and determination in getting herself fit as well as her horses, the cross-country phase of a Three Day Event is a big physical effort.

but each horse had gone well in one or more phases, which was what mattered, and with good going, well-constructed fences on a straightforward course and hours of unclouded but not too hot sunshine, it was an overall happy, friendly day.

By then Doublet was coming into the public eye. He had in fact qualified for Badminton in 1970, although there was no competing there because the Princess was away in Australia at the time. But various successes were making the pundits, and a section of the public, conscious of this horse that had learnt the sport step by step with his rider.

Different horses suit different riders, and where some people have an exciting effect on their animals, others have the reverse. Anne has the unconscious knack of relaxing hers, and needs a gay, strong and alert type of animal. And Doublet fulfilled all these qualifications, and more.

Speculation about Badminton the next year began to grow; the press

following pages: Many horses dislike jumping into water, but with Anne's determined riding Doublet jumped down into the hazard of the lake at Badminton and continued on his way without trouble.

25

had a feeling Prince Philip was not too keen on his daughter embarking on the gruelling world of Three Day Events; Anne, Alison Oliver and Doublet quietly went on training.

Excitement grew as the months drew on towards April 1971. Here was a member of the royal family entered for one of the toughest competitions in the world – would she get round? Had she got the right horse? Was her riding as good as some made out? And, of course, that hardy annual . . . are Three Day Events more suited to the physical strength of a man? Few seemed to consider the plain fact that if Princess Anne and Doublet had not been ready to compete at Badminton, they would not have done so.

Rushall in early April is the accepted 'school' for Badminton entrants. In the Open International Class, won by Mark Phillips and Ovation with a total of 38 penalties, Anne pipped him by one in the dressage for a 26, went clear in the show-jumping and put up an impressive but unhurried gallop across country to collect 22 time faults, and finish fourth.

Badminton began on April 22nd and finished on the 25th. Competitors came from Ireland, Holland, Switzerland and Sweden, and the British opposition was formidable – the holders of the Individual World and European Champion titles, Mary Gordon-Watson and Cornishman; Richard Meade, one of our most experienced riders; Lorna Sutherland with Peer Gynt; the consistently winning combinations of Mark Phillips and Great Ovation, and Debbie West with the little Baccaret; Richard Walker, always one to be reckoned with; Hazel Booth and the brilliant mare Mary Poppins; the list was long.

The royal family were out in force, the Queen, Prince Philip, the Queen Mother, Prince Charles and the two younger brothers, and

---

There's a lot more to eventing than just going all out to win and sometimes the requirements call for a lot of self-discipline – regardless – that is if one's sights are set on the heights. On this day at Crookham, in March 1971, Princess Anne and Doublet were in the lead after the dressage and steeplechase phases. But Badminton was only a week or so off, the cross-country was not of the type programmed for that stage in the training, and the Princess 'rode to orders' and withdrew.

In the line-up for her first Three Day Event, Princess Anne came fifth at Badminton 1971.

Princess Margaret all came along for the annual outing they much enjoy anyway, and to cheer on Princess Anne and Doublet at their first attempt at Badminton.

Anne scored 82.5 penalties for dressage, which left her in the lead at the end of the first day, and second to Mark Phillips' 75.5 in the whole competition. On the Saturday there were no troubles with roads and tracks, a minus 32.0, for time, on the steeplechase, and then it was out to the start of the cross-country.

The course was longer than the previous year, nearly the maximum permitted in an international event, a little more open and with more galloping. For the first time for some years it took competitors across the Luckington Lane, with a selection of new fences among the set pieces. A little rain would have improved the going, but the twenty-four-hour torrent that ensued produced very tricky conditions for the later starters, a sea of mud for the spectators, and a dreadful aftermath in his lovely park for the Duke of Beaufort to contemplate when it was all over.

Anne went off number 20 out of the forty-eight starters. No worries with fence number 1, tree trunks of 3 feet 9 inches; nor with the next, the woodpile, 3 feet 11 inches high with a 9-foot spread. Number 3 was The Coffin, a Badminton perennial combination – of 3 feet 6 inches rails followed by a jump-down over a 4-foot wide ditch, then up and out over rails at 3 feet 8 inches – that needs accuracy combined with impulsion, and that each year, including '71, causes a lot of trouble. But Anne and Doublet timed it neatly and galloped on to the Double Oxer, one of the biggest fences on the course, parallel bars and a hedge, 4 feet 10 inches high, making a 5-foot-9-inch spread, that has, as yet, never stopped anyone. Number 5, a zig-zag over a ditch, was the first obstacle that could be jumped in two ways – with a deep breath and straight ahead, or as Anne chose, with more discretion at an angle. The thorn hedge and post and rails that stood at number 6, at the first crossing of the Luckington Lane, also presented an alternative method of jumping, across the corner and was taken by a few with the nerve for a chance . . . and with the right horse. With the post and rails at 7 behind them, it was on to numbers 8, 9 and 10, the three 100-year-old, typical Beaufort stone walls called Tom Smith's Walls, that individually provide few difficulties, but as a combination call for control and obedience, and good riding rather than pure jumping ability, to avoid the overlapping penalty zones. Anne wasted no time, and then she and Doublet were sailing on over the natural fences of the second Luckington Lane Crossing, the thorn-hedge-oxer-rail-thorn-hedge of number 11, followed by the Bullfinch at 12.

The 13 feet of open water caused some trouble during the day – with the amount of rain-water lying about a few horses tended to treat it as just another puddle to be galloped through . . . with unfortunate results – but pushed on at it, and obedient to his rider's aid to take-off, Doublet was among those who took it in his stride. At the complex of ditch and rails called the Vicarage Vee, Doublet had a foot in the water and Anne had to sit tight as he half pecked on landing. There were no problems at the Vicarage Ditch or the Irish Bank with Rail at 7 feet, none with the Baby Elephant Trap or the Parallel Pen, a variation, using parallels, of the conventional enclosure to be jumped as an 'in-and-out' or as parallel rails. And so on to The Lake, and over 2-foot-9-inch rails with an extra drop into the water, and out again up a sleeper bank and rail at 3 feet 11 inches – the obstacle that, enlarged for an Olympic year and jumped the other way round was to give grief and a ducking to a number of competitors in '72. But Anne brought Doublet in steadily, slipped her reins to give him maximum neck stretch for balance, then pushed on with vigour, and they were out, on their way to the fearsome Normandy Bank, followed by the most spectacular fence on the course, the Ski Jump, a ramp with a terrifying 6-foot drop.

Number 21, the Normandy Bank, has a ditch in front of the 3-foot-9-inch bank, with 2-foot-3-inch rails over the exit drop. It has to be ridden with controlled impulsion and dash, and a rude shock awaited those who tried to hop on, take one stride and jump off again, as well as those who galloped flat out in a do-or-die attempt. Several competitors ended their cross-country phase at this obstacle, and, sadly, one horse was killed. Those who, like the Princess, combined determined riding with precise timing and a bold horse, made the bogey look almost easy.

It was the same with the Ski Jump. Come *too* fast, and your horse, caught completely off-guard may still have the ability to shout 'HELP!' and apply four-wheel brakes; come too slowly, and he'll slither to a stop peering with utter distaste at the depths below; come just right and it'll look simple . . . to the uninitiated.

Eleven more obstacles to go. No troubles with the Faggot Pile for all its 4-foot-9-inch spread, and nothing much to the Cattle Crush at 24 or the diagonal rail over a ditch that came next. No problems with the Sleeper Stack, although, looked at on foot, its width of 9 feet 2 inches seemed horrifying. Then, that other bogey, The Quarry, with two 'steps' down, one at 3 feet 8 inches, the other at 3 feet 10 inches, and out over nearly 4 feet of stone wall, all, once more, demanding a fairly slow approach but maximum impulsion. Safely through, six more to go – two lots of posts and rails, the Cat's Cradle with its alternatives, the more straightforward Huntsman's Close, with the cross rails over a ditch, at number 29, in between the two. End in sight – only the sloping tree trunks of the Knife Rest, then a plain Gate at number 32, and there's the Whitbread Bar to jump as the last fence and the welcome sight of the finishing post beyond.

There were no jumping penalties, only 32 for time, very few anxieties and a first-class round to put Anne into fourth place at the end of the day.

Sunday's jumping test was over an eleven-fence course, including three doubles and an open water. As might be expected the Princess and Doublet appeared a little tensed up, and there was an anxious moment at the beer barrel obstacle. Doublet cleverly got away with that, but had a foot in the water to collect ten penalties and drop a place from fourth to fifth.

So ended Anne's first Three Day Event. Fifth out of forty-eight, worth of rider and horse proved, enormous satisfaction and the sights now on Burghley.

Around a week later Anne was competing in the Windsor Horse Trials. Doublet was resting after his Badminton excursions and she took the field with Purple Star.

Purple, as always with a mind very much of his own, had ducked out at the gate and put Anne off at the qualifying event for the Foxhunter Championships a week before Badminton. He also thinks little of jumping into water, which is anyway an artificial occupation for any horse, and 'You'll have to push him hard!' warned Alison Oliver as they inspected the big jump into the lake at Windsor. Anne pushed with purpose, Purple responded with the spectacular leap he reserves for special occasions, and there they were . . . way out beyond the shallow landing zone, and actually swimming for dear life.

That's eventing for you, fifth at Badminton one week, swimming away from even a place among the finalists the next. And to add to it all, as Anne galloped by Alison, who was waiting at another fence, and shouted *en passant*, 'I've been for a swim!', she was not taken literally – not even when her soaked condition at the end of the course bore out the contention. In fact, it was not until the next day, when photographs in the Press appeared showing a not far short of totally submerged horse and rider, that Anne was able to prove her point incontestably.

CHAPTER EIGHT

Great hopes

AFTER Badminton, in the weeks before the selectors invited Princess Anne to compete as an individual in the European Three Day Championship, speculation about her chances of being chosen, and pressures in general, were rising. Anne herself, with Doublet having a well-earned rest until June, was fully occupied in her riding time, partly with Purple but principally with the two young greys, Columbus and Collingwood.

Way back in October '70 there had been rumours of a young horse of great potential at Brookfield. This was the giant 17.1, dappled-grey Columbus, that was joined not long afterwards by his full brother, the iron-grey Collingwood, younger by a year and smaller by a hand.

Both horses belong to the Queen, and both were bred at Sandringham out of the good mare, Trim Anne, that Princess Alexandra used to hunt, and sired by Colonist II, but their shared parentage has not produced similar temperaments.

Columbus is known, affectionately, as Monster, occasionally as Brute, nicknames easy to understand when, outside, he makes a not altogether playful grab at a passer-by or, with flattened ears and rolling eyes bangs on the bars of his loose-box and leaps up and down, daring one to enter. But go in quietly, ask him nicely how he does and request him politely to move over as required, and the 'fierce act' disappears as he complies. Fuss him, slap his side, which he hates, and say 'Get over, horse, I'm master here!' and he'll quickly try to prove you wrong, with more than a strong resemblance to his famous father.

Colonist II was a rough, tough old customer that sired many good jumpers and hunters. A new stallion man at Sandringham ruefully confessed to having been bitten, kicked and trodden on, all within the

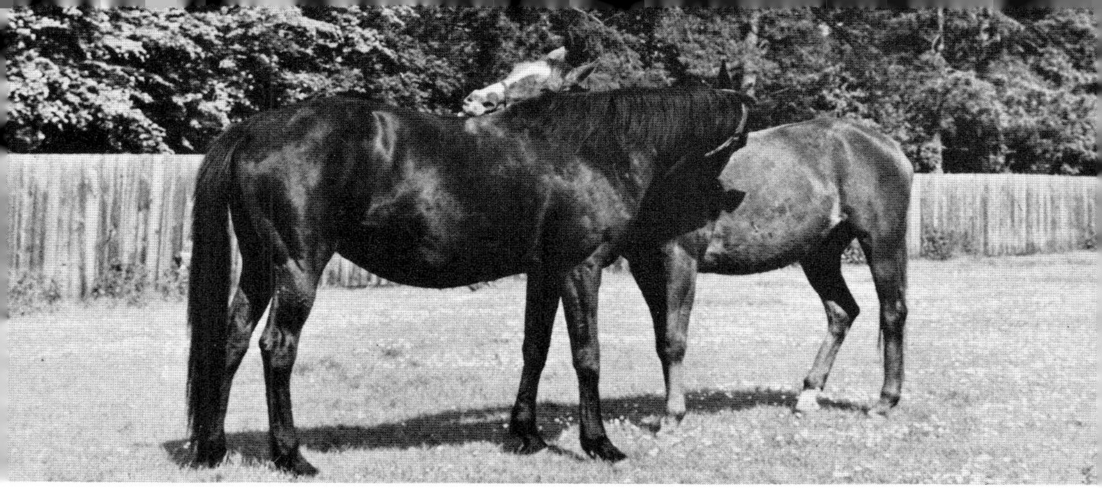

Trim Anne (*left*), was the dam of the Queen's young horses, Columbus, Collingwood and Mantilla, that are now ridden by Princess Anne. The mare, seen here with the Queen's Young Entry, indulging in a session of 'you scratch my neck and I'll scratch yours!', was the mother of many good riding horses, and at one time Princess Alexandra hunted her.

first week of taking charge of Colonist, and in the paddock he was one of the few horses that would not deviate when galloping towards you – and you had to do the getting out of the way . . . quick.

In his day the French-bred Colonist was one of the most popular of all racehorses. He belonged to Sir Winston Churchill – among his many successes was the appropriate win of the Winston Churchill Stakes – and he appealed particularly to the public for the great gameness, determination and stamina displayed in his running – characteristics Colonist shared with his owner. He was also an exceptionally bold horse, a trait that with his other qualities has been passed down to most of his progeny, and that is very evident in Columbus.

Neither of the greys are easy rides although both show, in rather different ways, a great deal of ability. For all his undoubted courage over fences, Columbus is excitable and highly strung, a horse that has to be treated with a great deal of tact and that is liable to 'boil up' at inopportune moments. He is also built on the lines of a strong steeplechaser, Grand National type, just the kind of animal the Queen Mother likes to own among her 'chasers. It was a royal family joke that Columbus must be kept out of her sight! In fact, by pure chance, she

Colonist II, one time famous and successful racehorse belonging to Sir Winston Churchill, was later for many years one of the Queen's resident stallions at the Sandringham Stud. He sired both the young grey horses that the Queen has loaned to Princess Anne, and has passed on much of his doughty spirit to Columbus and Collingwood – as well as some of the characteristics that made him a very tough personality to deal with!

did not set eyes on him until the King of Afghanistan came for a State Visit in 1971, and an evening parade of the Queen's horses was staged in his honour on the Indoor School at Buckingham Palace. Princess Anne and Alison Oliver brought Doublet and Columbus up from Bracknell to take part, and when the Queen Mother came to pat and take a look at Colonist's son, and made some joke about imagining she wouldn't get her hands on him now, she was told categorically that, no, there wasn't a chance!

The grey Columbus could have a great future in front of him. He has fantastic scope and a lot of ability, but has to be ridden with great tact and it is not easy to settle him sufficiently for the dressage phase. Here Princess Anne is jumping him across country at Tweseldown in 1971. In May 1972 she entered both Columbus and Purple Star in the Advanced section of the Spillers Combined Training competition at the Royal Windsor Horse Show.

By that year both young horses were appearing in public, once more with considerable success. In fact, by the autumn they had both upgraded to Intermediate, and by the spring of '72 Columbus was almost in Open.

At first Collingwood was the easier ride, partly because he was that much younger and not yet in his full strength, partly because he is a sweet-natured horse and basically tries very hard – even if this is not always apparent! He has always been a very relaxed mover, so that was no problem, and for that reason he looks nice when going, but by the spring of '72 he was getting a bit big for his boots, and almost more of a handful than Columbus, who was then coming out of a very difficult phase and beginning to settle – at least at intervals.

Collingwood, in fact, really upgraded too quickly, and he was still very green. Princess Anne felt that his resistance and penchant for slipping in the odd buck when asked to perform various movements, was part psychological – a Collingwood idea of a joke – but his conformation does not help. He is difficult to sit on, very springy in action and high in the back, one doesn't 'sit in' to him at all and both ends seem a long way off. He is rather a long horse, with a lovely 'front' but needing to 'make up' behind – as he will with time – and when asked by his rider to bring his hocks up under him, particularly in the small circles at the canter required in Intermediate dressage tests, he seemed to find it difficult, quite possibly a bit painful, and that made him stiffen. At the start it was found necessary to sit a bit forward in the saddle or he would immediately hump his back and buck – and it was better to make allowances, and not sit down on the 'hump' to try to force him when it started to come up, but to wait until he relaxed again.

In some ways Collingwood is more of a handful to cope with when he plays up than the bigger grey, and what he does is more complex, his resistance more cunning and less easy to sort out.

Columbus may try to evade the bit by over-bending, he may refuse

---

Collingwood, seen here at Tweseldown, is probably the easiest to hold of all Princess Anne's eventers, and she rides him in a plain jointed snaffle bit and a cavesson noseband.

to settle to dressage, as he did at the Windsor Trials in '72 – and in his early days it was sometimes impossible to keep him even within the bounds of the arena – but his efforts are usually a straightforward attempt to get going regardless, and one can at least hang on to him!

Both horses have a really big jump in them, and Collingwood is capable of putting up a first-class effort over show jumps for his stage in training, and went well in a Foxhunter class at Windsor in April '72, with only one fence down in the first jump-off. But where Columbus by that time was going like a lion across country, Collingwood was still demonstrating his greenness and an innate character trait, by liking to take a look first and jump afterwards, a habit that could not be pandered to and which sometimes made riding him across country uncomfortably exciting!

Anne found the education of her young greys both interesting and fun, but she did not find it altogether easy. Certainly it was no longer as it was in the early years, when a novice to eventing was finding her way with an equally novice horse and they learned together. Now an experienced rider was taking on, with Alison Oliver's help, the education of a couple of beginners. It was quite a hard task after the incomparable Doublet, a horse in a thousand, now a fully mature animal that knows his job, settles to each phase of an event as required, and has a totally co-operative understanding with his rider. Anne found she was inclined either to get 'scratchy' with the greys because they couldn't 'do a Doublet', and perform like him, or was alternatively too lenient, letting them get away with things because how could one possibly expect them ever to come up to him anyway!

By June '71 Doublet was in work again and obviously the priority, but Columbus and Collingwood were certainly not left out of the picture. It was still not certain whether the Princess would be asked to

---

Columbus is very big and strong and impetuous by nature. For jumping, the Princess uses the added control of a running martingale, attached to a breastplate that prevents the saddle slipping back. Columbus also wears a grackle noseband, a double noseband officially 'designed for a horse which "yaws", reaches for the bit with its mouth open, or swings its head'. In action here on the cross-country at Liphook, where they won the Intermediate Class.

ride at Burghley, but it was obviously on the cards and there could be no half measures about getting horse, and rider, fit. Training, with Anne giving every concentrated hour to it that she could, was in full swing when disaster struck, and the Princess had to go into hospital.

There was little time between the confirmation of the growing Press speculation that Anne *would* ride at Burghley, and the dashing of everyone's hopes with the possibility apparently nil. But she did, and she won; she proved that Badminton, which is often a law unto itself and can produce very unexpected results, had been no fluke. She became Individual European Three Day Event champion, was voted Sportswoman of the Year by the tough British Sportswriters' Association, with 123 votes ahead of the runner-up, and received two other awards of the same nature.

After the event was over Doublet was found to have bruised a tendon. In common with most of the other horses competing that day, he probably knocked himself on a fence in the cross-country, but it seemed of little moment.

The headlines started up again with a new, and obvious theme, OLYMPIAN LEAP FORWARD FOR ANNE? and the questions already started before Burghley gathered weight and momentum.

Of course it was the height of her ambitions to ride in the Olympics, to represent her country at Munich, and with her ability and this achievement, and with Doublet, now her very own, a present from the Queen after Badminton, and her urge to prove herself, how could it be otherwise? And she knew she could count on her family's backing –

---

above: Princess Anne and Collingwood – at speed on the cross-country course at Bucklebury. Balance and correct position of legs, body and hands adjusted according to the pace and requirements of the moment, are the secrets of good riding – and competing.

below: Another example of good riding – Princess Anne with Collingwood taking the log pile at Bucklebury Horse Trials in 1971. She is 'going with' her horse in perfect unison, weight forward, light contact with his mouth, and already looking ahead and riding Collingwood on to the next obstacle – all calculated to inspire confidence in a young horse.

and encouragement and pride – *if* it should come to having a chance of being in the team. But like the Queen and Prince Philip, Princess Anne is very much a realist. As she pointed out more than once, Munich was still a year off and there was a long way to go, and a lot could happen in the time. The results of Badminton '72, the 'pre-Olympic trial', would have to be known before the selectors compiled even their first list of riders and horses asked to go into special training, and the final selection would not take place until after another event only a few weeks before the Olympics. Just being a girl is a disadvantage when there are high officials in the eventing world with a sincere and professed preference for a male team; being a Princess was another.

For whatever Harvey Smith may, or may not have ill-advisedly thought or said on the subject of Princess Anne's qualifications as a possible Olympic rider, he was as much off beam in implying that she might not be chosen purely for ability, as he was in implying that a top-class show jumper is, of necessity, a top-class event rider.

If it came to selecting Princess Anne for the Olympics team, she would need just that much more ability than the next in order to be chosen – because subconsciously the selectors would be falling over backwards to ensure they were not influenced by her position. And although the fences in the show-jumping phase of an event must be easy meat for any top-ranking show-jumper, that does not mean he would necessarily be equally good at dressage or going across country. Both Soccer and Rugby Union are played with a large ball, and the players' feet and hands are used to good effect, but the hero of the FA Cup Tie is an exceptional man if he's also good enough at Rugger to play for England! Like eventing and show-jumping, the two sports call for quite a number of different skills.

After Burghley Doublet had nearly three months' rest, turned out at grass, and once again Anne was filling most of her riding time with Columbus and Collingwood, competing with quite a measure of success, and including the win of her section at the Holme Lacy trials with Collingwood that upgraded him to Intermediate. In October, as European Horse Trials Champion, the Princess appeared in the closing Cavalcade of the Horse of the Year Show, riding the show hack, Ridgewood Venture.

Hours of very hard work go into Princess Anne's successes at eventing. Even when she was preparing Doublet for Badminton in 1972, her young horses were not neglected, and the reward comes on such occasions as this – receiving her rosette for winning the Intermediate Class at Liphook, in that same year, with Columbus.

The weeks and months slipped by and it was time to start on Doublet's preparation for Badminton. It was disappointing that the slight thickening on his tendon, the result of the bruise obtained at Burghley, had not disappeared with rest as expected, but it did not seem to bother him in any way and the long fitness and training period commenced.

One of the chief arts of getting a horse fit is to time the peak for the right moment. If this looks like occurring too soon the work has to be curtailed so that the animal loses a little of its fitness, before being worked up towards the peak once more.

In the early stages Doublet's programme, like that of any horse being trained for a similar objective, consisted mainly of walking, but

Alison Oliver is a great believer in variety, and at all stages the day's routine would be based on avoiding boredom as well as on the requirements. Princess Anne came to work with her horse every day she could, and after she got back from the royal tour of the Far East, this meant three or more hours of solid work each morning, the time not spent on Doublet employed in schooling the two greys. She carried out whatever Alison decided would be right for the day – and this is how it always goes – and in the process of helping to get her horse fit became so herself.

Sometimes the work with Doublet would only take half an hour, or it would be two and a half hours in the paddock, mostly schooling on the flat to get him supple, obedient and relaxed, followed by some jumping over small fences or trotting over cavalletti. Some days they rode out at the walk for an hour and a half, then did an hour's dressage and ended with an invigorating gallop. And there was a great deal of walking, trotting and cantering up and down hills. Sunday was usually a rest day, unless there was a competition, when it would be transferred to Monday, and after these days off Doublet would prance out next morning quite a bit above himself.

The feeding was stepped up in ratio to the work. As he reached his peak fitness the oat intake should have been about 12–15 lb per day, but as often happens with horses at this time, Doublet became a bit finicky. He had no hay in the morning, but a big net at night.

By the beginning of April Doublet was looking a picture. Any superfluous fat had long been worked into hard muscle, his coat shone, his strange, pale-coloured eyes were bright and full of fire; he performed without effort anything he was asked to do, and was brimming with the courage and gaiety and controlled impulsion that makes Princess Anne feel he has no equal. But there was still a tiny niggle of doubt.

That thickening of the tendon had got no worse, it never 'filled' at night or caused the horse the slightest pain, but it was still there. Was it a weakness that might not stand up to Badminton? Could it give suddenly under the strain imposed by jumping over a course not far short of five miles? Might Doublet break down completely, injuring himself beyond repair?

Anne had taken him to Crookham on March 25th, where, for nineteen penalty points they performed perhaps the best dressage test of their career, and after a clear in the show-jumping, were in the lead at the end of the first day. They went clear also across country the next day, but it was not part of the programme to hustle along and they picked up 3 time penalties to finish eighth. No leg troubles, but then Crookham wasn't Badminton . . . and Badminton, which increases in severity during the years between the Olympics, was at the maximum in 1972.

It couldn't be left to chance, they had to find out one way or the other, and Doublet was taken on to Newbury Downs for a stiff workout that included a really hard gallop. That night Doublet's leg was 'up', but Alison, knowing that the Princess was in London with all her fingers crossed, kept hers crossed, too, and said nothing. If the swelling

On the steeplechase course at Cookham, Doublet showed no sign of the bruised tendon that was to dash Anne's high hopes.

should be down by morning it would mean it was of little or no consequence.

But the swelling was not down by morning and Doublet was obviously feeling it. Alison phoned the Palace, but Anne had a public engagement that day, and it was decided not to tell her until the evening that her luck was out.

CHAPTER NINE

Life and horses

It was a terrible disappointment, but it wasn't the shock it might have been. Anne had known for a while that it *could* happen, even if it was human nature not to believe that it ever really would. But for the time being it was the end of a dream, of an ambition, first sown at that Windsor Horse Trial six years before, that had gradually built up and materialised. And of course it wasn't only the finish to any thought of the Olympics in '72, it also meant no chance of taking on the field at Badminton and having a crack at doubling up on the big successes of the previous year.

Life seemed more than flat for a couple of days, but the Princess is never one to cry over spilt milk. Nothing could be done about it, it was just one of those things, and what was of most importance was that even if Doublet was out for that season, he wasn't permanently injured. Anne talked it through, then took the setback in her stride and got back to work with the other horses.

There was quite a bit of wishful thinking about Columbus – he had the ability to jump that course, if *only* he'd been entered. . . . It was a consoling speculation that would have gone down in family history as such, had not the Badminton committee decided actually to invite Princess Anne to compete with Columbus, *hors concours*, without contesting for a prize. And that of course altered the whole concept. What had been pure conjecture had now become a possible fact, and the papers took the idea up with enthusiasm. But the question had now to be squarely faced, was it really a good idea to take Columbus to Badminton at that stage in his career?

However tempting the offer, when it came to the crunch the answer had to be 'no'. Columbus had the scope, and because he is a horse that needs a great deal of exercise, he had been accompanying Doublet on all the fitness training and was supremely fit himself. But for all his potential, the big grey was young and his experience very limited, and the surest way to put a horse off jumping, maybe for ever, is to 'over-face' it at obstacles, or with a course, for which it is not yet ready. Only some little thing had to go wrong, a slip on a greasy take-off, or an over-jump that made it impossible to come out of a double without mishap, and Columbus' confidence and courage could, at that stage of

left : As she mounted Doublet at the Cookham Horse Trials in March 1972, Anne was not to know that this would be her horse's last outing for that season.

above : Princess Anne with Prince Philip at Badminton in April 1972 watching the cross-country where she had hoped to compete with Doublet.

his training, have received such a jolt that might have badly affected his future.

All being well, the big grey's graduated programme for the '72 season was to be the Two Day Event at Windsor, then possibly Tidworth, and, if things went according to plan, Burghley in the autumn. However alluring the thought, when it got down to brass tacks it could only have been silly to plunge him in at the deep end.

So, two days after knowing it was no Badminton, and while Doublet stood in his box, a kaolin poultice swathing the back of his tendon, Anne shook off the frustrations and took Collingwood to jump in a Foxhunter Class at Windsor. She was at Badminton on the following Saturday, an interested, wistful figure in headscarf and trousers, watching with Prince Philip, the fortunes, and misfortunes, of the forty-six competitors lucky enough to make the start. In the meantime and from then on, it was back to work, with eyes on the future and no retrospection, and with the Princess's dashing red Scimitar still headed for Brookfield on every possible occasion.

Each visit always began with a session for talking with Doublet the incomparable, with his aristocratic air and friendly, if slightly aloof approach. He had of course immediately had his high protein intake cut, and after a suitable diet of bran-mashes was eating, chiefly, hay and sweet grass, cropped outside for a while each day. His exercise was at first restricted to walking out in hand, but there is always plenty of other workable material awaiting Anne – behind the doors of the other loose-boxes.

There's little Purple, everyone's favourite, the perfect gentleman that holds his feet up as requested, has a taste for dandelions and is the recipient of more than his fair share of titbits. He is used for all and everything as required, but now holds the privileged position of an 'extra', plumper in figure than pure fitness would dictate, and coming into his own when the others are being rested. A little small for his owner now, for the 'big stuff', Purple is the perfect 'fun' horse, one who knows it all and will trundle off and do it – who loves to share the joke of his high spirits with Anne, and that's equally invaluable for working at home and practising things on, as for going to the odd competition, including advanced dressage.

Princess Anne takes her eventing seriously, but also derives the maximum enjoyment from training and competing alike. Riding has nothing to do with her role in life, and at Brookfield Farm she is free and happy in the relaxed atmosphere of which she is now a part.

There's the Queen's attractive bay, Mantilla, a half-sister to the two greys, also out of Trim Anne but sired by the Thoroughbred Manicou. Then she was only a four year old, still only a baby, quiet to handle and quite a bold jumper, with a little of the 'family' temperament. At only 16 hands the mare is likely to be a bit small for the Princess's eventing requirements, but has the stamp and potential of a first-class dressage horse.

And of course there's always as much time as possible to spend on Columbus and Collingwood. It may start off with the bigger of the two, for an hour's concentrated schooling indoors. No exclusiveness about this – a couple of Jack Russell terriers may be hunting mice noisily among the straw bales at one end of the school, and Columbus, when he appears to be in a receptive mood, is perhaps asked to attempt

left and right: On this occasion Collingwood and Columbus were still two of Anne's promising young horses. Within a very short time Columbus in particular was to become her chief hope for the 1972 season.

a half-pirouette while another rider canters by, or fit in a 15-metre circle around another pupil having a lesson from a mounted instructor. But whether it's tracking left and right, halting, backing, a rising or a sitting trot, ordinary canter, extended canter, canter from the walk, the team work never stops. Alison notes it all, the right, the wrong, the improvement, the evasion, while Anne, quick to interpret the suggestions, works on them until progress is achieved or, occasionally,

and in respect to the grey's mood of the moment, by mutual agreement it seems best to leave well alone until another time.

Then it's back to the stable, undo Columbus's 'boots' and take off his bridle while one of the girls saddles up Collingwood, and then it's clomping off up the road to the jumping field.

There the larks shiver up into the sky where at intervals the jets from near-by Heathrow thunder overhead, and the easy collaboration continues. Alison sets up the fences and decides what to do, then assesses the results as Anne takes the jump. It's all relaxed and without tension, there's no attempt at big fences, the objective is to get the

Princess Anne communing with Collingwood. She has a great *rapport* with her horses – talks to them, shares jokes with them, 'cusses' them at intervals, but very seldom gives them any of the blame when things go wrong competing. To be on such a wavelength is to enjoy the full happiness that can come from companionship with a horse.

horses athletic and correct, in approach and execution, over small obstacles and combinations, but there's a lot of hard work involved. There's been an hour or more of concentrated schooling before this, there may be a ride out or more schooling to come. In the meantime there are suppling canters for obedience in between the jumping, perhaps Purple comes up for a session too, and there's probably an unwinding, twice-round-the-field gallop to finish with.

After it's all done with for that day, while Columbus is led in after being sponged down and grazed, after Collingwood has been 'undressed' and is being rubbed down in his box, while Doublet and Mantilla watch as Purple gets down to roll, then stands to shake throwing up his bedding like chaff, Anne climbs into her car and roars off back to Windsor or to Buckingham Palace.

Riding, and the horses, and Brookfield are only a part of Princess Anne's busy life, but they are important. As fourth in succession and Second Lady in the Land, her job entails public duties and spending much of her time in the public eye. As a member of the royal family, the Princess accepts this as part of her job and would hate to feel she was not pulling her weight, but like all public figures she needs an absorbing hobby, and as much freedom as is possible for one with her role in life.

This is what the horses can provide for Anne, and with them she has been able to prove herself to herself. No doubt she will be taking on all-comers at Events for a long time yet, and given the luck should be in a position to be chosen in due course to defend her European title, or aim for even higher conquests.

It's more than probable that by next, the 1973, season, Anne will be in the enviable position of being able to compete with two top-class horses, Doublet and Columbus. It's obviously impossible as yet to judge just how much rest Doublet's leg will require, and certainly he'll not be hurried back into competing until he's ready; but even if he's not tried out in the spring competitions he should be perfectly fit for those later in the season. And since Columbus' only real problems are his strength and impetuosity, which are both good faults in an Eventer, he looks to have a great future. Collingwood, if without quite his brother's scope, continues to improve and do well. There are also Mantilla, who is coming along nicely, and possibly other young horses to work on, Purple always ready and willing for anything required of him, and High Jinks and Royal Ocean for pleasure-riding at home. In competitions at all levels the Princess is now acknowledged as a great competitor, single-minded and determined to win – but one who never loses sight of her horse as a partner in the effort. Nor does

left: Anne and Alison Oliver discuss Columbus' efforts during schooling.

above: Dressage is usually Columbus' bugbear, but at Tidworth in May 1972 Anne and he were leading in the dressage of their Rover section, but his impetuosity cost them dear on the cross-country. Columbus could be one of the big hopes for the future, but is a problematical character.

she lose sight of what she owes to Alison Oliver. Above all, she always has the innate desire to ride well, and achieves this through dedication, a good, adaptable seat, natural balance and rhythm, a cool head and the enviable, rare gift of 'hands'.

Whether Princess Anne and her horses have further, higher fields to conquer remains a matter for the future, but with them, if certainly without conscious effort, she provides her own generation with a fine example of courage and sheer 'guts'. And with it all, in the company of Doublet, Purple, Columbus, Collingwood, Mantilla and any other young ones that come along – and never forgetting Jinks – Anne has a great deal of fun.

Acknowledgements

The author and publisher wish to acknowledge with thanks permission to reproduce the photographs appearing on the following pages:

p. 23: reproduced, by gracious permission, from *The Queen Rides* by Judith Campbell, published by Lutterworth Press

Front cover, pp. 26 (above), 27, 33 (above), 41, 70 (above and below), 102: Godfrey Argent, reproduced by gracious permission, from *The Queen Rides* by Judith Campbell, published by Lutterworth Press

pp. 26 (below), 33 (below), 34, 36, 38, 39, 46, 53, 55 (left and right), 71, 101: Godfrey Argent, reproduced by gracious permission

pp. 75, 77, 78: BBC

pp. 66, 84, 85, 88 and 89, 124, 125: Central Press Photos Ltd

pp. 92 and 93: Gerry Cranham

pp. 31, 59: Crown copyright, by permission of Cassell & Co. Ltd., photographer Nicholas Flower

p. 122: *Daily Telegraph*

p. 94: Keystone Press Agency Ltd.

pp. 113, 116, 120, 121: E. D. Lacey

Frontispiece, pp. 6, 12 (above and below), 16, 51, 56 (above and below) 103, 105, 106, 108 (above and below), 111, back cover: Leslie Lane

p. 63: *Leicester Mercury*

pp. 21, 25, 28, 45: *London Express*

pp. 30, 67, 74, 81: John Scott

pp. 65 (above and below), 91: *Sport and General*

pp. 83, 119: *The Times*